The Language of Postcolonial Literatures

This book provides a comprehensive introduction to some of the central features of language in a wide variety of postcolonial texts.

Many international works of literature in English cannot be divorced from their connection to British imperialism. In *The Language of Postcolonial Literatures*, Talib argues that this connection is being challenged by postcolonial writers. The book draws on a range of writers, from Jean Rhys and Derek Walcott to Chinua Achebe, Ngũgĩ wa Thiong'o, Nuruddin Farah and Salman Rushdie, to show how English has been shaped by and has had to contend with other languages in former British colonies. Exploring literatures from a range of countries, including India, Nigeria, Canada, Australia, Scotland, Wales, Ireland and the Caribbean, Talib shows how individuals retain cultural and national identity in the face of such changes. The book further demonstrates that language is one of the central concerns of postcolonial literatures.

The Language of Postcolonial Literatures is invaluable for anyone with an interest in the evolution and development of English and its use in contemporary world literatures.

Ismail S. Talib is an Associate Professor at the National University of Singapore.

The Language of Postcolonial Literatures

An introduction

Ismail S. Talib

London and New York

First published 2002 by Routledge
11 New Fetter Lane, London EC4P 4EE

Simultaneously published in the USA and Canada
by Routledge
29 West 35th Street, New York, NY 10001

Routledge is an imprint of the Taylor & Francis Group

© 2002 Ismail S. Talib

Typeset in Baskerville by
Prepress Projects Ltd, Perth, Scotland (www.prepress-projects.co.uk)
Printed and bound in Great Britain by
TJ International Ltd, Padstow, Cornwall

British Library Cataloguing in Publication Data
A catalogue record for this book is available from the British Library

Library of Congress Cataloging in Publication Data
Talib, Ismail S., 1955–
    The language of postcolonial literatures: an introduction/Ismail S.
Talib.
        p. cm.
    Includes bibliographical references (p.) and index.
    ISBN 0–415–24018–2 (hardcover) – ISBN 0–415–24019–0 (pbk.)
    1. Commonwealth literature (English) – History and criticism.
2. Nationalism and literature – English-speaking countries.
3. Nationalism and literature – Commonwealth countries.
4. Language and culture – English-speaking countries. 5. Language
and culure – Commonwealth countries. 6. Postcolonialism – English-
speaking countries. 7. English language – Commonwealth countries.
8. Postcolonialism – Commonwealth countries. 9. Decolonization in
literature. I. Title.

PR9080.5 .T35 2002
820.9'9171241–dc21   2001051055

Contents

Acknowledgements

This book could not have been written without the help, example, precedence and inspiration of many people: creative writers from the postcolonial world, scholars of their writings and colleagues and friends.

In writing this book, I am immensely grateful to the following scholars for their valuable ideas, informativeness and resourcefulness in research: Helen Gilbert, Joanne Tompkins, Bruce King, Feroza Jussawala, Reed Way Dasenbrock, John Skinner, Dennis Walder, Robert Crawford, Jane Wilkinson, Stuart Hall, Graham Huggan, Gareth Griffiths, Helen Tiffin, William Walsh, Elleke Boehmer, David Westley, N.F. Blake, Maya Jaggi, Ania Loomba, Ben Anderson, Marshall McLuhan, Richard Bailey, Stephen Slemon, Raka Shome, Peter Young, Bill Ashcroft and Michael Wilding.

I should also mention the following scholars and critics, whose ideas and observations have helped me to tie the various strands of the book together: Makarand Paranjape, Susan Van Zanten Gallagher, Kirsten Malmkjær, Denis Donoghue, D.S. Izevbaye, Biodun Jefiyo, Braj Kachru, David T. Haberly, Ali Mazrui, Sachidananda Mohanty, Meenakshi Mukherjee, Harish Trivedi, George Yancy, James Munson, Juliet Okonkwo, Kenneth Ramchand, Gauri Viswanathan, Anandam Kavoori, Paulina Alberto, James Wood, T.J. Cribb, Arnold Rampersad, Everett Emerson, Douglas Barbour and Paula Krebs.

This book would not have been realised without a number of friends and colleagues who have encouraged me and provided me with valuable suggestions or ideas, both before and during its writing. I would like especially to mention Ron Carter, who suggested that I should write a book of this nature some years ago. Kirpal Singh has been a faithful friend and inspiration throughout the writing of this book. I am immensely grateful to Bill Ashcroft and John McRae, who read an earlier version of the book and made some valuable suggestions. I would also like to mention colleagues or former colleagues at my Department in

Singapore who have helped me in various ways: Walter Lim, Barnard Turner, Anthea Fraser Gupta, Peter Tan, Koh Tai Ann, Rajeev Patke, Kay O'Halloran and Edward McDonald. Last (but certainly not least), I would like to thank Louisa Semlyen, Katharine Jacobson, Christy Kirkpatrick and the language editorial staff at Routledge, without whose untiring help and interest in the project this book would literally not have come into being.

Ismail S. Talib
November 2001

1 English in (post)colonial contexts

England colonised and the importance of Latin

In the past, England has been a colony. For nearly four centuries it was ruled by Rome. The last time there was a successful invasion was in 1066, when it was conquered by the Normans. Although England might have been independent after the Norman conquest, 'it doesn't compensate for [its] shocking home record' up until then, as it was 'rolled by the Romans, Vikings and various Germanic tribes in quick succession' (Thompson 1998: 6; see also Carter and McRae 1997: 5–6; Hunter 1997: 543–5). One of the invading Germanic tribes introduced into England what was to become the English language. Thus, the language closely associated with England (or earlier versions of the language) only emerged after the Romans had left. The close connection of the English language to colonialism can thus be seen from two different angles: it spread throughout the world partly as a result of British colonialism, but was itself introduced into Britain as a result of invasion.

Latin and English language and literature

Latin continued to be a very important language in Britain long after the Romans had left. Indeed, it has a longer presence in Britain than English itself, which was only introduced after the Roman withdrawal. The continued importance of Latin, and the belief that it was more intrinsically expressive as a literary language (Jones 1953: 3–21), led many later English writers to write literature in that language.

Latin was a highly prestigious second language during the Norman French occupation (when contrasted with the lowly third language of English) and was used for religious and scholarly work. It was also used as the language for public worship until the middle of the sixteenth century. Indeed, so unimportant was English in England, especially in the first two centuries of Norman occupation, that there was a real danger that the language would simply die out (Dorian 1981: 2).

The belief that literature should be written in Latin remained long after the Norman French occupation. Among writers who wrote in Latin were famous English language poets, such as Andrew Marvell and John Milton. Milton even thought of writing what was to become his great epic poem *Paradise Lost* in Latin, but fortunately for the English language he changed his mind.

As a language that continues to be important after the collapse of the empire connected with it, English may now be playing a similar role to Latin. The English language and its literature today continue to grow after the demise of much of the British Empire, which is a situation that was seen earlier with regard to Latin. It is therefore ironic to note that English suffered earlier in its history as a result of the post-imperial importance of Latin. As Vincent Gillespie pointed out to Ngũgĩ wa Thiong'o on his visit to Oxford University, there are 'interesting parallels' between Ngũgĩ's concerns with the dominance of English over languages such as Ngũgĩ's mother tongue Gĩkũyũ, and 'those of people like John Trevisa and others who used to fight for the independence of English from Latin and French' (Ngũgĩ 1998: vii).

The English language, as Ngũgĩ (1998: vii) aptly reflects, has itself 'gone through a post-colonial phase'. The turning point came in the sixteenth and seventeenth centuries, when there was 'a postcolonial/ colonializing dynamic ... in which the English came to think of themselves and their language both as having been colonized and as potentially colonizing others' (Helgerson 1998: 289). From the seventeenth century onwards, the colonializing tendency gradually became more prominent, and today, even though the British Empire is no more, the language is still spreading across the globe.

The survival of Latin, however, unlike that of English, was partly sustained by a belief in the intrinsic superiority of classical languages. Because of their classical pedigree languages like Latin and Greek were, for a long time, regarded as intrinsically superior to other more recently developed languages, such as English. The supposed superiority of Latin led some seventeenth-century grammarians of English to think that English should be based on Latin grammar, in spite of some significant grammatical differences between the two languages. This view may seem anomalous today, but it became influential, and was to have an effect on the teaching of English grammar until the early part of the twentieth century. The supposed intrinsic superiority of Latin also led some poets in English to try to use quantitative metre for the writing of English poetry, in which metrical *feet* are measured in terms of long and short syllables. But the sounds of English resist the dominant metre of Latin poetry. The survival of English had a more practical bent, but as will be seen later in this chapter, there have been views expressed, although less persistently than with regard to Latin, that it is intrinsically superior to other modern languages.

Ethnicity, nationality and language: a linguistic confusion

The word 'English' refers to both ethnicity and language. Its double meaning underlines a complication that is still with us. The word *English* also has a link to *nationality*, viewed in terms of residence, a sense of belonging to a community, or the citizenship of an existing political state. The last definition of nationality, at least at present, is questionable, as the political unit that matters with regard to citizenship is Britain and not England. In general, English literature is less often formally defined in terms of nationality. However, as will be seen shortly, nationality is in fact an important criterion in the attempt to define what *English literature* is. Whatever it is, the criterion of nationality to define English literature may not be helpful, but may actually increase the likelihood of more confusion.

The ethnic and linguistic split indicated by the word *English* is pretty obvious to us: although it is not common for an English person not to speak English at all, there is no logical contradiction if this happens. On the other hand, it does not mean that only an English person speaks English, as there are millions of non-English speakers of the language today. In any case, the word 'English' is arguably less confusing today than the words 'French' or 'Russian', which, in addition to language and ethnicity, are also defined in terms of citizenship. However, 'English' may suffer the same fate as 'Russian', as regards the additional definition of the word to refer to citizenship. The word 'Russian' to mean 'citizen of Russia' became a reality after the collapse of the Soviet Union. In the same vein, the possibility that the word 'English' will refer to a citizen of England instead of Britain may be realised after the comprehensive devolution of Northern Ireland, Wales and Scotland.

The distinction between language and ethnicity, or the decrease in the importance of language as a factor in defining ethnicity, may result in the search by the historically original speakers of the language for some kind of ethnic 'essence'. The identity of an ethnic group which carries the language's name becomes more difficult or elusive because its language has become internationalised. What results is an *identity* problem created by the split between race and language. In the case of the English, the identity problem may be linked to the search for the essence of 'Englishness', and the extent that it should be linked to the language. This identity search is exacerbated by the decline in the political and economic power of Britain. As Terry Eagleton has noted:

> Englishness has never really needed to be defined before, at least in the good old Imperial days. I think the need for national definition is felt more by the underdogs, who have to define themselves against the dominant forces.
>
> (quoted in 'The Way We Are')

Effect on literary studies

The definition of the word 'English' is not merely a semantic consideration. In addition to its effect on political or cultural studies, it also has an effect on literary studies, for it touches on the question of what *English literature* is, and what should and should not be included within its reach. This, however, does not mean that its definition will draw the boundaries of English literature with extra clarity. John Skinner (1998: 7) has noted that the word 'English' lacks the distinction, for example, between ' "Arabic literature" (or literature written in the Arabic language) and "Arab literature" (literature written by Arabs)'. In a similar vein, Latin literature 'refers objectively to literature written in the Latin language rather than literature written by "Latins" ' (Skinner 1998: 25). Although ' "English literature" may yet come to refer primarily, if not exclusively, to literature written in the English language, rather than literature produced within a specific area or by a particular ethnic group' (Skinner 1998: 26), that time has not arrived. The central question that needs to be asked is whether the term English literature should be defined in relation to language, ethnicity, or nationality.

Today, English literature is seldom simply defined in terms of the use of language, as this would include all literature written in English across the world. It is also not defined in terms of the ethnicity of the writer, as this would exclude writers who are not ethnically English, such as Joseph Conrad, or, for that matter, writers such as Oliver Goldsmith and Walter Scott, who were Irish and Scottish. It would also have to include writers who are ethnically English but who do not reside in England, and hence embraces many writers from the British Commonwealth and the United States.

Thus, in the attempt to define English literature, the lowest common denominator is writers resident in England. However, there are immediate difficulties with this definition, as it has to be extended to include writers from the other British countries: Wales, Scotland,

Northern Ireland and, for a period in British history, the whole of Ireland as well. So, given what has been passed off as 'English literature' in schools and universities, all British writers are included. However, this definition is inadequate in one important respect, which was touched on at the beginning of this book. As Saldívar (1997: 159), citing Raymond Williams, has reminded us, 'In the English context, ... there were at least fifteen centuries of native writing in other languages: Latin, Welsh, Irish, Old English, Norse, and Norman French'. So it does seem that the linguistic criterion has to be brought back, but only with reference to writers who are resident in Britain. For writers writing in English but who do not reside in Britain, it is generally agreed that the term *literature in English* is more appropriate.

Relativity of power and dominance: a strand in postcolonial theory

This chapter began by saying that even England had been colonised, that the English language itself was introduced into Britain by invading forces and that people who were ethnically English were once reluctant to use their language, especially for the writing of literary works. These assertions were not made to excuse British imperialism in the past. Neither were they an attempt to excuse the continued dominance of the English language today. One reason for beginning with them is to highlight the relativity of power and dominance – be it linguistic or political. This relativity is an important strand in postcolonial theory, and will play a vital part in many of the arguments in this book. In this regard, what is once central is no longer regarded as such, and vice versa. With reference to the writing of literature in English, it has been argued, in another context, that the use of the English language by those originally on the 'margins' (for example, by writers of literature outside Britain) has now resulted in the appropriation and dismantling of 'the model of centre and margin' and 'the notions of power inherent' in being at the centre (Ashcroft *et al.* 1989: 83). Thus, what was at the margin of English is now at the centre.

Dominance of language and literature may be determined by extrinsic forces

Feelings of the inferiority of a literature may be justified if they are wholly based on the intrinsically negative value of the language and literature, which is always difficult to prove with any degree of objectivity. However, the belief in the inferior position of a language and its literature is often determined by extrinsic factors. Specifically, the rise of the use of English and its literature has to do largely with factors external to both the language and its literature. The same can be said about the dominance of Latin and classical Greek language and literature several centuries before the rise of English, in spite of claims to the contrary.

Nevertheless, there were some Britons who believed in the intrinsic superiority of English by claiming that their language was 'the finest and purest spoken' (Alberto 1997). This view extended to English speakers outside Britain, such as the American poet Walt Whitman, who believed that 'the English language is by far the noblest now spoken – probably ever spoken – upon this earth' (quoted in Bailey 1991: 110). If it was not seen in such superlative terms, it was perceived to be a far superior language to the language of those who were colonised by the British. The missionary Cotton Mather, for example, believed that 'the English Tongue would presently give [the American Indians] a Key to all our Treasures and make them the Masters of another sort of Library than any that ever will be seen in their Barbarous Linguo' and that they 'can scarce retain their Language, without a Tincture of other Salvage Inclinations, which do but ill suit, either with the Honor, or with the design of Christianity' (quoted in Bailey 1991: 73). Moving to Africa in the twentieth century, it was claimed, in a report published by the British Colonial Office in 1953, that 'without the English language to generate a correct set of values in Africa, the continent would collapse into "moral confusion and lack of integrity" ' (Alberto 1997). Thus the teaching of English falls in line with the dubious civilising mission of colonialism (see p. 8).

However, although there have been many claims concerning the superiority of English (see also pp. 12–13), not many people have claimed that English literature itself is superior to other literatures in the world. The claim that European languages and literatures as a whole are superior to other languages and literatures is more often made. The latter claim came into prominence with Macaulay's notorious minute on Indian education (1835). In it, Macaulay (1952: 722) stated his belief in the 'intrinsic superiority of the Western literature', and that 'a single shelf of a good European library was worth the whole native literature of India and Arabia'. Later scholarship has cast serious doubts on the basis of such judgments. It has been argued, for example, by Martin Bernal in his book *Black Athena* (1987) that certain important aspects of Greek civilisation itself, which was the first civilisation in Europe, were of African origin.

British expansion and the spread of English

There is no question that the spread of the English language had to do with the rise of British imperialism. This was not a unique situation, as the spread of other European languages around the world, such as Spanish and French, also had to do with the rise of Spain and France as imperial powers. The close relationship between language and empire was recognised right from the start of Western expansion. In 1492, for example, the Bishop of Avila said to the Castillian Queen Isabella, when she was presented with a book of Spanish grammar by medieval linguist Antonio de Nebrija, that 'language is a perfect instrument of empire'.

Britain and the British Isles

Before going further in the discussion on the relationship between English and the British Empire, a distinction must be made between Britain and the British Isles. *Britain* (soometimes known as Great Britain) is a political entity, whereas *the British Isles* is a geographical entity that includes England, Scotland, Wales and Ireland. Ireland (sometimes referred to as Southern Ireland), as it is an independent political entity, is not included when referring to 'Britain'. The term, the *British Isles*, is widely used, and will be used here, even if it is unfortunate that the word 'British' in the *British Isles* is taken from the root word 'Britain'. However, when the word 'British' is used by itself, it is an adjective derived from the word Britain, and hence is used to describe a political entity or someone's or something's association with it.

The rise of British imperialism

The British Empire began in the late sixteenth century. In the seventeenth century, sugar and tobacco plantations were established in the Caribbean and in the south-eastern part of what is now the United States. During the middle of the century, Britain expanded into India and Canada. At the end of the century, although it lost the American colonies – which were to form the United States of America – further colonies, such as Ceylon, British Guyana, Malta and the eastern coast of Australia, were added to the empire. Between the seventeenth and eighteenth centuries, Britain expanded further into India, Africa, Asia and Australasia. Eventually, between the end of the nineteenth century and the beginning of the twentieth, the British Empire was spread over about a quarter of the land mass of the world. At its height, it was one of the largest empires in the history of the world. After granting independence to the colonies, unity among the ex-colonies was voluntarily maintained by the Commonwealth of Nations, which was founded in 1931.

The civilising mission of colonialism

Colonialism has been described by the colonists as having a civilising mission, in the sense that the colonised stand to benefit from it in educational and social terms. Joseph Conrad's *Heart of Darkness* (1902) is a classic text on the pitfalls in the belief in colonialism's 'civilising mission'. Although it refers to Belgian colonialism in Africa, it could quite easily have referred to British imperialism in general: the references to London in the novella make the association quite clear. There were many who believed in colonialism's civilising mission. To some, the belief was dubiously couched in Darwinian terms. In Krebs's (1997: 429–30) description of this tendency, there was the prevalent view that 'Africans were lower on the evolutionary scale than Europeans and in need of guidance, direction, and encouragement so that they could eventually reach the Europeans' level'.

Language and empire

Language had a part to play in the expansion of the British Empire and the continued unity of the British Commonwealth. The Empire was of course responsible for the initial spread of the language. During the rise of the British Empire, the associated spread of the English language had to contend not only with Latin but also with European languages of the other imperial powers, such as French and Spanish, which are still important international languages today. However, Britain, in comparison to France and Spain, had the biggest empire, and, furthermore, colonised the United States, which in its own right was to become an important force for the spread of English. Both these factors ensured that English was as widespread as the two other imperial languages. In some senses, the spread of English today may be more extensive than the two other languages. English is the main language of commerce and of science and technology, and more people study it.

English has been viewed as a potent force for the assertion of command and control in the Empire. Paulina Alberto (1997) made the claim, for example, that 'Britain's most powerful battle standard in its competition for the domination of new continents against local inhabitants was Standard English'. A case in point is the belief expressed in print by the British philologist William P. Russel in 1801. Russel argued that:

... if many schools were established in *different* parts of Asia and Africa to instruct the natives, *free of all expense*, with *various premiums of British manufacture* to the most meritorious pupils, this would be the best preparatory step that Englishmen could adopt for the *general* admission of their commerce, their opinions, their religion. This would tend to conquer the heart and its affections; which is a far more effectual conquest than that obtained by swords and cannons: and a thousand pounds expended for tutors, books, and premiums, would do more to subdue a nation of savages than forty thousand expended for artillery-men, bullets, and gunpowder.

(quoted by Bailey 1991: 106–7)

Thus, educating the natives in English not only served the civilising mission but also – and more importantly perhaps – the imperial mission of exerting better control over them.

The fall of the British Empire

As noted earlier, the breaking up of the British Empire left a linguistic residue which may eventually last longer than the Empire itself. In the words of Minette Marrin (1998: 26), 'We may have lost an empire, but we have gained a lingua franca'. The continued significance of English after the demise of the British Empire has been mentioned at the beginning of this chapter. However, too much significance should not be attributed to the British Empire as a factor contributing to the spread of English, as 'the supremacy of English may have much more to do with the American empire than with the British' (Marrin 1998: 26). Nonetheless, the United States itself was once colonised by the British, and if it was not for this fact, English might not have been as important in the United States today. Thus, even if the focus is to shift to the United States, the historical importance of the British Empire in the spread of English cannot be denied.

The rise of literature in English and the Empire

English literature can be said to have spread together with the expansion of the English language. What began as the spread of English literature later resulted in the growth of literature in the language, written by non-English writers. The attempt to view these developments in a positive light did not end with the collapse of the British Empire. In fact, there is now a retrospective process, whereby the worldwide spread of literature in English is taken as a justification for British imperialism in the past. Of course, we can quarrel with the 'argument' on strictly logical grounds. Nevertheless, Robert Hanks (1997: 25) has expressed the view that 'a strong point in ... favour [of the British Empire] is the vast body of literature in English that it produced.' He elaborates:

> [The status of English] as lingua franca of the largest empire the world has yet known means that writers and readers from opposite ends of the earth can be introduced to one another without worrying about what's getting lost in the translation – Flann O'Brien and Salman Rushdie can have a common audience. And these writers have the advantage, as it seems to be, of writing in a language that is both their own and not their own: they are native speakers, but they have, perhaps, an awareness of the language's individual quirks and an ability to work against the grain that come harder to writers who are simply English.

The above 'justification' for British imperialism is perhaps more commonly encountered in relation to the English language itself. Gaurav Desai (2000: 523), for example, who came from India and lectures on English literature in the United States, encounters not only awkward remarks about 'how well' he speaks English, but, on occasion, the further remark that 'the British really knew what they were doing when they taught Indians their language'.

English literature and the Empire

In the attempt to use the worldwide spread of literature in English as a justification for British imperialism in the past, it has been controversially claimed that 'one of the great tributes to the British Empire, and to the intrinsic quality of our literature, which obviously needed an empire to spread it, was that Arundhati Roy's *The God of Small Things* is written in English' (cited by Marrin 1998: 26). Roy was present when this sentiment was expressed by the historian Edward Chaney, and was not pleased at all. In Marrin's words (1998: 26):

> Arundhati Roy's novel is in English because English is her element. It is her first language; it is 'the skin on my thought', she says, and 'the way I think'. Clearly she loves it. Using English both in speaking and in writing obviously gives her immense joy. ... And yet she speaks English only because it was imposed on her; it was imposed on her forebears by conquest, imposed on her immediate family by all kinds of painful social and religious identifications and interests, and imposed on her by them.

So the relationship of Empire to English literature, and subsequently, to literature in English, can be said to be ambivalent, and cannot be wholly seen in a positive light. According to Roy, 'being forced to identify with a conqueror, especially with a departed conqueror ... "is like being the child of a raped mother" ' (Marrin 1998: 26).

Spread of the Empire led to the spread of English literature

David Armitage (1998: 99) has noted that 'English Literature and the British Empire were the twin children of the English Renaissance' The literature grew with the Empire, and at 'the height of the British Imperial power, the relationship between literature and empire seemed self-evident' (Armitage 1998: 99). In spite of the close connection between literature and Empire, Britain did not have an epic poem on imperial expansion comparable to the *Lusiads* (1572) by Camoëns, which is a narration of Portuguese imperial expansion led by the explorer Vasco da Gama. If anything, some earlier British writers were quite critical of colonialism.

The spread of English Literature was also accelerated by its use in the classroom. The extension of English literature as a subject to be taught in schools went hand in hand with the rise of British imperialism. Literature was not merely taught for itself, but served a tacit ideological function. By 'the early twentieth century, students across the Empire were being instructed as to the world-excellence of English literature and Western rationality, and the deficiencies of their own' (Boehmer 1995: 170).

English literary education in India, for example, was a way of imparting hidden quasi-Christian religious values to Indians (Viswanathan 1989). It championed the ideal Englishman and was concomitantly a means through which Indians could become estranged from their own culture. Through the educational process, they would readily accept British culture and domination. The teaching of English literature in Indian schools was in fact carried out, after the English Education Act of 1835, long before it was done in British schools.

The spread and growing prestige of the English language had to do with the Empire, and, at least with regard to giving it the initial push, might have also enhanced the prestige of English literature. Thus its prestige remained after independence of the colonies, and also had a contributory effect on the prestige of literature from England, which was believed to represent the best usage of English. This is reflected, for example, in the teaching of literature in the language in the United States, where the belief that 'access to English Literature gave access to "proper" language – and so to power – explains the popularity of the subject of Rhetoric and Belles Lettres in North America' (Crawford 1992: 39).

Superiority of language and dialect

One of the notions explored in the philology of nineteenth-century Europe was the superiority of the European languages when compared with the other languages of the world. But even within Europe there was a hierarchy of languages, and English was originally not as well thought of as it is today. The classical languages, Latin and Greek, as noted earlier, were once regarded as superior to modern languages such as English. However, this view underwent a change in the eighteenth century, with some views being expressed that English had a superior position among the modern languages because of its intrinsic qualities. This was the view of Macaulay, whose view on the superiority of European literature was mentioned above. With specific reference to English, Macaulay (1952: 722) has this to say in his 1835 Minute on Indian education:

> The claims of our own language it is hardly necessary to recapitulate. It stands pre-eminent even among the languages of the west. It abounds with works of imagination not inferior to the noblest which Greece has bequeathed to us; with models of every species of eloquence ...

Perhaps the most prominent of the views that English was a superior language because of its intrinsic qualities was made by Jakob Grimm in an address to the Royal Academy of Berlin in 1851. According to Grimm:

> Of all the modern languages, not one has acquired such great strength and vigour as the English. It has accomplished this by simply freeing itself from the ancient phonetic laws, and casting off almost all inflections; whilst from its abundance of intermediate sounds [*Mitteltöne*], tones not even to be taught, but only to be learned, it has derived a characteristic power of expression such as perhaps was never yet the property of any human tongue ... Indeed, the English language, which has not in vain produced and supported the greatest, the most prominent of all modern poets (I allude, of course, to Shakespeare), in contradistinction to the ancient classical poetry, may be called justly a LANGUAGE OF THE WORLD: and

seems, like the English nation, to be destined to reign in future with still more extensive sway over all parts of the globe.

(S.H. 1853: 109–10)

Other positive views on English have been mentioned earlier in this chapter. However, these views may not extend to English as a whole, as there is a perceived hierarchy of dialects of the language, some of which are regarded as being more prestigious than others.

Purity and socio-economic considerations

When compared with classical languages, not only was English ranked lower in its early history, but it suffered from the perceived problem of not being a 'pure' language. Although generally recognised as a Germanic language, English is a compound of several languages, especially when it comes to its vocabulary, and includes many Latin and Norman French words. The high ranking given to the classical languages in philology was not determined by politico-economic factors, but more by a romantic belief that language is 'purer' the earlier it is in its evolutionary development.

However, the counter-argument that English is superior because of its very mixture is not only possible, but has been put forward by, amongst others, the American poet Walt Whitman (1982b: 1165):

> View'd freely, the English language is the accretion and growth of every dialect, race, and range of time, and is both the free and compacted composition of all. From this point of view, it stands for Language in the largest sense, and is really greatest of studies. It involves so much; is indeed a sort of universal absorber, combiner, and conqueror.

Purity of dialects

A similar view is also held of certain dialects of English: that the further one moves backwards in time, the 'purer' it was, and therefore superior, or at least more praiseworthy, when compared with dialects that developed later. Therefore, dialects that are able to maintain some ancient features are regarded as purer and superior to those that are not able to do so. For example, it has been argued that 'some isolated communities (for instance, in the east-central United States) are "explained," and thereby approved, as retaining qualities of

"Elizabethan English" ' (Bailey 1991: 125). Moving closer to England, some of the Scottish dialects of English spoken in the Highlands are believed to be 'purer' varieties of English, as they are closer to older varieties of English than contemporary varieties of English spoken in England itself. The claim that the dialects are closer to an older variety of English is of course open to analysis, and whether this ensures the 'purity' of the dialect is open to question, as it cannot be scientifically verified in a systematic way.

Ranking of dialects of English

Although the maintenance of old features is a factor in the ranking of dialects, it is difficult to separate language and dialect from socio-economic considerations. The development of what is regarded as 'good' or 'standard' English is a case in point. Its development, especially with regard to pronunciation, was determined by the socio-economic dominance of certain regions within England itself. It is important to clarify this matter here, as what constitutes 'good English' plays a prominent part in the colonial linguistic attitude towards the literary use of other dialects of English to be discussed in the next chapter and in the rest of this book. Colonial linguistic attitudes are present internally, within England itself, and are later transferred to the English and literature in the language of the other nations of the British Isles, and to the world at large.

The norm of what 'good' or 'standard' English is, is derived from one of the dialects of English spoken in south-eastern England, which was relatively wealthier than other parts of England. The elevation of the southern dialects of English is not a new phenomenon. According to Bailey (1991: 26) 'the notion that "good English," the sort associated with important public business, was southern' was believed to be there from the end of the fourteenth century. Even at that time, an important indirect factor that influenced people's linguistic evaluation was the fact that the north was generally poorer than the south. Not all southern dialects are highly regarded of course. In Alexander Gil's study of British dialects, *Logonomia Anglica*, which appeared in 1619 and 1621, the Somerset dialect is described as 'barbarous'. Gil may have been influenced by the depiction in Elizabethan drama of the south-western dialect of English as peasant language (Blake 1981: 94). Yet again, the economic factor plays a part here, as the south-west was poorer than the south-east. In this regard, the Scottish writer Alasdair Gray (1990: 31), among others, is right in pointing out that what is recognised as standard English is simply another dialect of English, and, for a long time, it was 'the main dialect of the British rich'.

There were also external considerations coming from outside England itself, which contributed to the rise of what was considered standard English. In this regard, it has been quite persuasively argued by Alberto (1997) that a good case can be made that the rise of the notion of what standard English should be developed more outside England than within it. To her, the development of this notion came hand in hand with the rise of British colonialism. Alberto specifies that the notion of what 'King's English' is might have arisen as a reaction to the threat of foreign corruption of the language. Thus 'King's English' is defined negatively by fears of what English should *not* be rather than what it is or should be. Another external factor is the international prestige value of the variety of English that the British themselves hold in high regard. It has been noted by Richard Bailey (1991: 124), for example, that even when the variety of English spoken outside England 'is fully established (as in the case of modern American, Canadian, New Zealand and Australian Englishes), there remains a persistent belief that the prestige norms of south-eastern England still provide a model for the "best" English, at least for some purposes.' It seems clear that there are both internal and external factors that converge towards the promotion of the south-eastern dialect of English as standard English.

In addition to notions of what 'good' or 'standard' English should be, there is a hierarchy of dialects in Britain, with the perception that the more prestigious dialects are associated not only with higher social and economic status but with higher intelligence as well. In Britain, a certain Glaswegian dialect is regarded as prestigious (not the Glaswegian dialect Kelman portrays in his work!):

> In the vast majority of cases, the accent is perceived as being of a slightly higher calibre than most regional UK accents. Even the residual of a Glasgow accent is preferred to the residuals of Birmingham or Liverpool. There's a perception of people being better educated and more intelligent in Scotland.
>
> (Ewan Gowrie, cited by McAlpine 1996)

However, a person's perceived socio-economic status may be determined by the dialect or accent used, and not by his or her job or assets. As noted by the novelist Will Self, 'What defines you as being working class [in Britain] is having a regional accent – of whatever kind' (Barnes *et al.* 1998: 170).

The attitude towards the less prestigious dialects is also carried over to their use in literature. This attitude is sometimes criticised as being connected to linguistic imperialism, a criticism which is increasingly levelled against England within Britain itself. Here, for example, are the views of the Scottish novelist James Kelman, with reference to the attitude towards his use of language in fiction:

> The problem with any term like 'idiom' or 'vernacular' used about my work is that it appears to be a euphemism or synonym for 'language'. I try to say at all times, let's just call the Scottish working-class way of speaking a language.
>
> The rejection of it as a language is to do with imperialism and the language of the coloniser. This is the idea that every other culture and therefore language is going to be defined against it. The way we use language is seen as being a debased form of English.
>
> (quoted in 'Capturing Working Scots' Idiom')

Postcolonial attainment of prestige

However, Kelman's attitude towards language does not reflect the belief that there is no such thing as 'standard' English in Scotland. There is the perception there that there is a distinctive variety or dialect found in Scotland, which can be regarded as the 'standard' for Scotland, quite distinct from the standard English of England. Attainment of independence, or of some kind of self-determination, may result in more prestige being accorded to this standard variety of Scottish English. For example, the linguist Jeremy Smith believes that a Scottish parliament, which became a reality again in 1999, could boost the prestige of Scottish Standard English (cited in McAlpine 1996).

The canon and postcolonial literature (s)

In spite of the difficulty of establishing English literature itself as a viable and respectable body of texts, the works belonging to the literature became canonised once literature became institutionalised as a subject taught in schools and universities. For example Saldívar (1997: 157) notes that 'When I first arrived at Yale as an undergraduate in the early 1970s, the English department believed it was its business to teach the canon of English and American literature'. Once works of mainstream American and British literature are canonised, it is difficult to challenge them. Canonisation does not help the newer works and as many of the works in postcolonial literatures in English are relatively new, they were introduced into the curriculum only with some difficulty and resistance. Since they are not directly associated with England, postcolonial literary works face a further difficulty, especially with

English literature programmes that take a more holistic approach to the subject by including courses on British society and history. This more holistic approach to the study of English literature may not be congruent with the context for the study of postcolonial literatures. Unless it is modified by the more extensive inclusion of the history of British colonial expansion outside Britain, it may actually make it more difficult for postcolonial literary works to be introduced into the curriculum.

Definition of postcolonial literature(s)

Postcolonial literatures can be defined as literature written by colonised and formerly colonised peoples. This should include literatures written in various languages, and not only in the language of the colonisers. This is the simple definition that will be taken as the starting point. Although the approach here will be to concentrate on the English language, this is not intrinsic to the term *postcolonial literature*.

Anglocentrism and Eurocentricism

Although the use of English is not intrinsic to the term *postcolonial literature*, it needs to be noted that when the term is used to refer to the literatures of countries colonised by the British, it is too often taken to refer to literatures in English. According to Aijaz Ahmad (1992), this Anglocentric tendency smacks of theoretical imperialism. This is a situation accidentally created by the fact that much of the early interest in postcoloniality arose among scholars specialising in literature in English. The bias towards English has in turn created an irregularity that needs to be adjusted, as noted, for example, by many researchers of postcolonial Indian literature:

> It is indeed true, as Harish Trivedi, Arun Mukherjee, and G.V. Prasad point out, that only texts written in English/english merit consideration as 'postcolonial' texts within the discursive framework set up by definitions of postcolonialism emerging from and published in the West. This is surely an egregious mistake especially concerning India, where superb texts both ancient and modern written in innumerable regional languages far outnumber those written in English.
>
> (Afzal-Khan 1998: 221)

A further problem is the term *postcolonial* itself, which seems to centre the discussion of history on Europe. According to Kavoori (1998), 'the singularity of the term effects a recentering of global history around European time'. Not only does it privilege Europe, but to Meenakshi Mukherjee, it unjustifiably focuses attention on the English language:

> The term post-colonial tends to confer a central position to one century of European imperialism in the long narrative of the human race, making it the determining marker of history, and without ever stating it in so many words, invests the English language with a measure of presence and influence that is somewhat out of proportion to what statistical or demographical facts would warrant.
>
> (Mukherjee 1996: 8)

Binary oppositions

One of the difficulties frequently discussed in postcolonial theory is the rigid division of the world into two categories: the West and the East, the North and the South, the developed and the undeveloped, the First and Third Worlds, the English and the non-English. Undoubtedly, binary categorisations of the world may have positive aspects or consequences. Ashcroft *et al.* (1995: 8), for example, have rightly pointed out that 'the binarisms of colonial discourse' may help postcolonial critics to 'promote an active reading which makes ... texts available for re-writing and subversion'.

Whatever the merits of the binary divisions, however, the world is not so rigidly divided. There are, for example, some parts of the so-called 'Third World' which cannot be regarded as postcolonial, not because they have been influenced by the First World, but because they have not been touched by colonialism. Meena Alexander sees this in India:

> India is currently a post-colonial society but then of course there are people whom colonialism has never touched. In fact, it is totally irrelevant to their experience. So, is their experience 'post-colonial'? Well, I don't know.
>
> (quoted in Mohanty 1997)

This does not mean that such binarisms can be dismissed completely. It has been mentioned above that binary categories may have positive aspects or consequences. Moreover, they may, in a sense, be impossible to discard, as they may rhetorically be needed in order to talk or write on the postcolonial condition. Dismissing them completely may result in a lack of clarity or systematicity in presenting one's arguments, even if there is a denial of the reality of the situation as it should be. Indeed, the charges of Anglocentricism and Eurocentricism discussed above, which are legitimate, are based on just such a binary classification of the world. Binary categories have been used and will continue to be used in this book, but with some qualifications where necessary. What is essential is the recognition of their limitation, deficiency or equivocation, and they should not be presented as if they are immaculate and clear-cut representations of reality.

Problem with the 'post-'

The problem of the definition of 'postcolonial' may be focused more on the prefix 'post-', which implies that something is 'over' or completed. According to Loomba (1998: 7), 'it implies an "aftermath" in two senses – temporal, as in coming after, and ideological, as in supplanting'. It is its definition of 'aftermath' in the conceptual sense that Loomba finds more contestable: 'if the inequities of colonial rule have not been erased, it is perhaps premature to proclaim the demise of colonialism'. The non-temporal definition of the 'post-' in postcolonial is not new. Gallagher has reminded us of Fanon's definition of the term, in which 'the postcolonial is never a specific moment but an ongoing struggle, a continual emergence' (1997a: 377).

However, there are still some critics who insist that the 'post-' here has a temporal denotation. One of them is Anandam Kavoori, who defines it as such, and makes an objection to it, as colonialism has not ended. But it has been pointed out that Kavoori's understanding of the prefix 'post' is mistaken, or is, at best, a minority opinion in postcolonial studies. According to Raka Shome (1998: 204), 'the prefix "post" used in such theoretical vocabulary does not mean a final closure, nor does it announce the "end" of that to which it is appended; rather it suggests a thinking through and beyond the problematics of that to which it is appended.'

There is the prevalent understanding that the 'post' does not mean 'after' in the temporal sense or conceptual sense. This understanding is present even among academics who cannot be classified as postcolonial scholars, such as Walter Laqueur (1995: 32), to whom postcolonial theory refers to the belief that 'imperialism had, and continues to have, a negative impact on the colonial world'. According to Viljoen (1996: 63), if colonialism 'is defined as the way in which unequal international relations of economic, political, military, and cultural power are maintained, it cannot be argued that the colonial era is really over'. Indeed colonialism may exist side by side with postcolonialism. In this regard, Viljoen (1996: 63) cites the view of Ashcroft *et al.* that postcolonialism is 'a potentially subversive presence within the colonial itself' and not really separated from it by coming after it.

2 Anti-colonialism in Scottish, Welsh and Irish literatures

One of the paradoxes of British colonialism is that it enabled the colonised to use the English language, which was in turn used in the nationalistic struggle against the colonial masters associated with the language. This type of nationalistic anti-colonialism may manifest itself in literature written in English. In the words of Bruce King, colonialism brought with it not only the English language, but 'English literary forms, and English cultural assumptions' as well (King 1974: 2). But as King has rightly pointed out, these imports can be turned on their heads, especially if there is the feeling that 'the English cultural tradition is no longer relevant outside the British Isles' (King 1974: 2). As will be seen later in this chapter, this reaction also applies to cultures which are found indigenously in the British Isles, and not only to those which are remote or significantly different from the English.

England is not Britain

England is only part of Britain, but the two are often confused. Another confusion is the view that the English are the overwhelming ethnic group and culture in Britain, to the complete exclusion of the other cultures and ethnic groups, including indigenous ones. This view, of course, is quite common outside Britain, and is even prevalent in scholarship at the international level. Robert Crawford (1992: 10), for example, has correctly noted that among 'the international array of contributors' to the book *Nation and Narration* edited by Homi Bhabha, 'only Gillian Beer seems to have a clear and explicit awareness that the words "England" and "Britain" are not synonymous'.

The assumption that Britain and England are similar is not only found outside Britain, but is also very much alive within England itself. Within England, Ann Leslie has noted in a newspaper report that:

> The English have tended to use the terms English and British synonymously. We [the English] were the boss nation, the dominant culture, and the Celtic fringes were merely colourful add-ons to the prevailing English, sorry, British way of life.
>
> (Leslie 1998: 22)

Her view is an echo of the observation of the Anglo-Welsh poet and nationalist, R.S. Thomas, to whom 'the UK is only a euphemism for England' and that '[t]he Scots, the Irish, the Welsh are just appendages' (Jury 1997). With specific reference to English poetry, John Lucas (1990: 3) observes that 'when English poets speak of Britain as a nation of the free they usually mean England'. This confusion works to the political advantage of the English, and the disadvantage of the Scots, Welsh and Irish.

Literature in English by the non-English in Britain: I

When it comes to the history of British literature, the fact that literature in English can be written by the Scots and Welsh, and not necessarily by Englishmen, is virtually a platitude. However, English was not the only indigenous language of the British Isles, and the indigenous literatures of Britain need not be in English. These facts are very often less noticed, largely because of the prevalence of the English language today. The overwhelming dominance of English obscures the visibility of these other indigenous languages of the British Isles.

Hostility towards England

Today, and in the past, the indigenous non-English peoples of the British Isles often display hostility towards England and the English, for they believe that the politically dominant English and their language will destroy or corrupt their own language and culture. Some of these sentiments have found their way into their literatures. For example, between the twelfth and fourteenth centuries, some poets in the Welsh language, which is a Celtic language distinct from English, were calling upon their fellow Welshmen 'to seize the throne of England, and thereby to restore honour and glory to the Welsh people' (Parry 1955: 158). It did seem to them that only by counter-conquest could the respectability of the Welsh and their language and culture be revived. These sentiments are still current today. The twentieth-century Welsh-language poet Gwenallt Jones, for example, is described as having a 'settled hostility to England' as he believes that it is 'for ever threatening to stifle and obliterate the language and culture of Wales' (Parry 1955: 416).

Another reason for their hostility is the supercilious attitude of the English towards the non-English indigenous groups in Britain. Some of these groups are viewed as having barbaric customs which have no place in modern society, but which they have not quite discarded:

> The tribal ceremonies of the peoples of the British Isles are bewilderingly vulgar. I once attended a banquet in London which was interrupted by Scots pipers marching round the tables, going full blast in bearskins and kilts. An Italian next to me assumed it was a terrifying student prank. When I reassured him he replied: 'But I thought our Julius Caesar had helped you wipe out these people.'
>
> (S. Jenkins 1997)

If the 'tribal' people of Britain (which would supposedly exclude the more civilised English) are not regarded as barbaric, then they are regarded as quaint, and therefore, when contrasted to the English, inconsequential. In this regard, Ann Leslie (1998: 22) has again observed that:

> [To the English, the Celtic] fringes had charming accents and were good at things like making porridge, booze and male voice choirs, but Celtic nationalism itself – a sense of belonging to a separate 'race' – was regarded as somewhat childish. On a par with all those tedious Yorkshiremen who say, 'I'm a Yorkshireman and proud of it!', Celtic nationalism was regarded as the sort of bombast you get from people with a rather deserved inferiority complex.
>
> We felt (in so far as we thought about it at all, which was scarcely ever) that to be born English was to have won the first prize in the lottery of life.

The 'Anglo-' prefix

As literature in the Welsh language continues to be written, the term 'Anglo-Welsh literature' may have to be used to refer to literature in English written by the Welsh. Although it has been said by the Anglo-Welsh poet John Davies in his poem 'How to Write Anglo-Welsh Poetry' that 'Being Anglo-anything is really tough' (cited by F. Jenkins 1997), and that some people object to the prefix because of 'the kind of cultural hybridity it implies' (Skinner 1998: 276), it is clear that the term cannot be avoided. *Welsh literature* without the prefix may very well mean literature in the Welsh language. The same can be said about Irish literature, where it has been noted that many Irishmen 'do not regard anything written by their countrymen in English as Irish literature' (King 1974: 16). The term 'Anglo-Irish literature' is thus used for related reasons, even though literature written in English constitutes 'the dominant literary tradition of the nation' (King 1974: 16). By extension, the same situation applies to Anglo-Scottish literature.

In short, the convergence of ethnicity and language is certainly there with the word *Welsh*, and arguably, with the words *Irish* and *Scottish*. So the terms *Welsh, Irish* or *Scottish literature* may indicate literature written in the respective Celtic languages. The prefix *Anglo-* is thus simply linguistic, and the terms *Anglo-Welsh*, *Anglo-Irish* and *Anglo-Scottish literature* may be more precise indicators that the literature is written in the English language.

However, the use of the Anglo- prefix is not merely a semantic consideration, as it also has a connection to nationalism. The situation is more clear-cut in Ireland when compared with Wales or Scotland. The feeling of colonisation was, and still is, strong in the island of Ireland as a whole, but especially so among the Catholic community in the north. It is also strong, it should be emphasised, in Scotland and Wales, and cannot be dismissed, even if it has been, in the past century, historically less violent than in Ireland.

Although Scottish nationalism had been historically less intense than Irish and Welsh nationalism, it has been noticeably strong in recent years, and present in contemporary Anglo-Scottish literature as well. The intensity of Scottish nationalism today may possibly lead to the independence of Scotland from the United Kingdom. Indeed, if Scotland and Wales are considered together, it has been predicted that nationalism in these states may eventually lead to the termination of the United Kingdom itself in the second or third decade of the twenty-first century (Miller 1998).

Literature in English by the non-English in Britain: II

Literature in English in England is also written by authors of non-indigenous descent. They, or their parents, emigrated to England from the former British colonies. Many of them are rightly considered as postcolonial authors, because they continue to write about the countries they left behind, and to bring along with them certain assumptions about Britain from the eyes of the colonised. They have not fully assimilated themselves into England, and their sense of separation does not make them completely belong to the community of English authors. Indeed, authors such as Wilson Harris, Salman Rushdie or Buchi Emecheta have often been regarded, respectively, as Indian, Caribbean (more specifically, Guyanan) or Nigerian authors as well.

These authors are important in the contexts of both literatures in English and British literature. Harris, Rushdie and Emecheta, together with V.S. Naipaul, Ben Okri and David Dabydeen among others, form a significant group of authors who cannot be neglected in the recent history of British literature (see, for example, Carter and McRae 1997: 488–9, 526–30). Naipaul has been aptly described by Carter and McRae (1997: 529) as 'the grand old man British literature', and the influence of Rushdie on contemporary literatures in English, not only in England and India but worldwide, cannot be underestimated. Rushdie was the winner of the Booker of Bookers in 1993 for his novel *Midnight's Children* (1981). Rushdie has also been described (Wong 1996: 200) as letting the novel in English go *jungli* (which is the Hindi expression for going 'native'). As most of these authors will be discussed in other regional or national contexts in future chapters, this chapter will concentrate on authors who are less likely to be discussed in these other contexts, such as R.S. Thomas and James Kelman.

Scottish, Welsh and Irish literatures

Scottish, Welsh and Irish literatures were of course once unequivocally treated as 'English' literature. From one perspective, this may be correct: as these literatures were written in English, they should be regarded as part of 'English' literature. Indeed, it has been asked, 'Is a poet from Wales writing in English any different from an English poet?' (Jenkins 1997).

However, the word 'English', as seen above, has several meanings, and there is an inherent ambivalence between ethnicity and language. Because of this ambivalence, the view that Scottish, Welsh and Irish literatures should be regarded as 'English' literature is by no means uncontroversial. Moreover, the other nationalities of the British Isles may actually regard English as a foreign or alien language, and not as their own language. This view may occur even among those who use English very well, and write literary works in it. For example, in an oft-quoted passage towards the end of James Joyce's *Portrait of the Artist as a Young Man* ([1916] 1960), the main character, Stephen Daedalus – who has a command of English, but not of Irish Gaelic – notes the difference between his English and that of the Dean of Studies:

> The language in which we are speaking is his before it is mine. How different are the words *home*, *Christ*, *ale*, *master*, on his lips and on mine! I cannot speak or write these words without unrest of spirit. His language, so familiar and so foreign, will always be for me an acquired speech. I have not made or accepted its words. My voice holds them at bay. My soul frets in the shadow of his language.
>
> (Joyce [1916] 1960: 189)

In the words of T.J. Cribb (1999: 107), Stephen 'feels provincial, inferior and dispossessed' when using English, in spite of his good command of the language.

Stephen Daedalus's comment is by no means an isolated one in other respects. The first national literature in English in the British Isles to question its status as part of English literature was Anglo-Irish literature. Irish literature had an important, if indirect part to play in the eventual attainment of Irish independence. As noted by Cribb (1999: 108), Irish literary nationalism proclaimed and carried 'into *de facto* effect a cultural independence before political independence was possible'. This is the pattern that the Scots, and to a certain extent the Welsh, are trying to emulate. At present, there is a growth of nationalism in Scotland and Wales, which has led to the interrogation of their literatures in English as part of *English* literature. Even before devolution from Britain became a serious issue in Wales and Scotland, the increasing consciousness of internal colonialism in Britain should eventually lead to the view that these literatures are to be treated separately (Thomas 1971).

Nationalism in these literatures

One distinguishing feature of contemporary Scottish, Welsh and Irish literatures is the unmistakably stronger sense of nationalism in them when contrasted to literature written by the English. Perhaps the English do not know, owing to the overwhelming dominance of their culture, what there is to be nationalistic *about*. The stronger nationalistic tendency in these literatures has been noted by, among others, Julian Barnes:

> Is there a connection between literature and a sense of nationalism among the countries in the United Kingdom? Clearly in the case of Scotland, Ireland and Wales. Nationalism in England is less straightforward, more reactive and less likely to express itself through literature.
>
> (Barnes *et al.* 1998:174)

However, at a simple level, nationalism in Scotland, Wales and Ireland may also be regarded as reactive, in the sense that it is a reaction to England and the English. With reference to Scotland, for example, it has been noted that 'A lot of people when asked what it means to be a Scot will reply in effect that it is not to be English' (Massie 1998). Nationalism in these states may also be a reaction to the disintegration or diminution of Britain as it was known several decades ago. As noted by Andrew Neil (1998: 11):

> There was no conflict about being both [British and Scottish] in the Scotland in which I grew up and was educated in the Fifties and Sixties. The mood is very different today: the past two decades have seen the rise of an increasingly separatist Scottish identity and a concomitant decline in British identity north of the border.

But quite evidently, there is more to their nationalism than a mere negative reaction to the English, especially when referring to their literatures. A.S. Byatt, for example, has 'the impression that the Scots, the Northern Irish and the Welsh [when contrasted to the English] do have both strong literary communities and a strong sense of national literatures' (in Barnes *et al.* 1998: 174). Their nationalism may be due to the relatively stronger desire to define their cultural identity. In this connection, the editor of *Poetry Review*, for example, has remarked 'that whereas Scots, Irish and Welsh writers never stopped thinking about their cultural identity, modern English poetry was short on self-analysis' (Scammell 1998: 13).

Problems with nationalism in literature

One problem with nationalism, especially in relation to contemporary British literatures from outside England, is that perhaps the appropriate word to use, according to Salman Rushdie, is *nationism* rather than *nationalism*. In this regard, Rushdie (1997b: 22) has some pertinent observations to make on the Anglo-Welsh poet, R.S. Thomas. Rushdie quotes the following lines from Thomas:

> Hate takes a long time
> To grow in, and mine
> Has increased from birth;
> Not for the brute earth ...
> ... I find
> This hate's for my own kind ...

In relation to these lines, Rushdie (1997b: 22) notes:

> [It is] Startling to find an admission of something close to self-hatred in the lines of a national bard. Yet this perhaps is the only kind of nationalist ... nationist ... a writer can be. When the imagination is given sight by passion, it sees darkness as well as light. To feel so ferociously is to feel contempt as well as pride, hatred as well as love. These proud contempts, this hating love, often earn the writer a nation's wrath. The nation requires anthems, flags. The poet offers discord. Rags.

So the 'nationist' poet gives something more negative than the generally positive vision usually imparted by nationalism.

While recognising the presence of nationalism, especially in discussing the literatures from a postcolonial context, it is also important to realise that there are problems with this label in teaching and criticising the literature. For example, when Denis Donoghue (1997) was teaching the works of Jonathan Swift at the University of Cambridge, 'I didn't make much', according to him, 'of his being Irish'. According to Donoghue, Swift's 'styles concerned me more than his nationality or his version of nationalism'. In general, Donoghue is against the belief that: 'We are to approach a work of literature only for its symptomatic value as an illustration of some attitude already at large in the rhetoric of Irish identity'. As an example, he picks the analysis of Yeats's *Leda and the Swan* in Declan Kiberd's *Inventing Ireland*. According to Kiberd, in Donoghue's words, Yeats's poem is 'simply a poem about England's "rape" of Ireland'. However, the 'poem remains intact' in Donoghue's view, 'only because the commentary leaves its literary qualities untouched'. Thus too much interest in nationalism, to Donoghue, may deflect attention from other qualities found in the work.

Anglo-Irish, -Scottish and -Welsh literatures as postcolonial literatures

Anglo-Irish literature

William Butler Yeats, one of the great twentieth-century poets writing in English, was a senator of the Irish Free State. Indeed, Irish literature in English boasts some of the best-known writers in what is often termed *English literature*. Looking at the twentieth century alone, there were James Joyce and Samuel Beckett. Although less overtly involved with politics when compared with Yeats, their writings can also be viewed in a postcolonial context.

Joyce, for example, has been aptly described as 'a central figure for many of the post-colonial writers in English because of the way he comes to the English tradition as an outsider and bends the English language to fit his Irish subject matter and language' (Jussawala and Dasenbrock 1992: 15). It is in this light that Joyce has been recently seen as a postcolonial author (Mays 1998), with his final novel *Finnegans Wake* (1939) – which, in the best postcolonial spirit, puts 'standard English to sleep' (Kiberd 1999) – as an example *par excellence* of how the language of the colonial masters can be used as a weapon against them. Joyce and the text of *Finnegans Wake* are certainly seen as such by Terry Eagleton (1995: 269): 'Joyce turns the medium of English against the nation which nurtured it, thus reversing the colonial power relation at the level of discourse ... In thus estranging the English language in the eyes of its proprietors, he struck a blow on behalf of all of his gagged and humiliated ancestors'.

Beckett went in a different linguistic direction: he stopped writing original works in English, and went on to write them initially in French, and to translate some of them into English later. Beckett's development can in fact be compared to that of the Kenyan writer Ngũgĩ wa Thiong'o, who will be mentioned again later in this book: after writing some novels in English, Ngũgĩ eventually abandoned English as a first language for creative writing, and wrote in Gĩkũyũ.

Towards the end of Joyce's novel *Portrait of the Artist as a Young Man,* the main character, Stephen Daedalus, after feeling alienated from the English language itself, becomes preoccupied with the idea of exile, and contemplates the prospect of banishing himself to mainland Europe. This was the path taken by Joyce himself. Beckett was also a voluntary exile in Europe. He spent much of his life in Paris. Because Beckett initially wrote many of his works in French, he is also regarded today as a French author.

It must be stressed that Yeats, Joyce and Beckett are Irish authors, even if they are often included in English literature courses. So important are they as writers in English that the need to create a separate category of Irish literature, or Irish literature in English, in order to accommodate them does not often arise. As major writers, their exclusion would be at the expense of a balanced English literature programme. It can also be argued that Ireland only achieved full independence from Britain in 1949, after the deaths of Yeats and Joyce. Beckett is less often included, although one is not sure whether this is because many of his works were produced after 1949, because he is regarded more as a French author, or because he is regarded as a lesser author than Yeats or Joyce. However, Irish independence in 1949 was merely formal, as Ireland had regarded itself as virtually an independent state, with a parliament of its own, for several decades before that.

Anglo-Scottish literature

With Welsh and Scottish literature, however, the distinction from English literature is less clear, although, like the Irish, some Welsh and Scottish writers have been nationalists. The major Scottish poet of the twentieth century for example, Hugh McDiarmid, was one of the founders of the Scottish National Party in 1928. What can best be described as anti-colonial sentiments have certainly not been watered down in recent years, and this is clearly seen in the views of some of the more recent Scottish writers. In some ways, these sentiments have actually grown. For example, James Kelman (1997: 13), 'felt an immediate kinship' when he 'first read *The Palm Wine Drinkard* in the early 1970s … as when I read Sam Selvon's *Lonely Londoners*'. *The Palm Wine Drinkard* (1953) is by the Nigerian author Amos Tutuola, whereas Sam Selvon was originally from Trinidad. Kelman is of the view that recent Anglo-Scottish literature is 'a radical literature', and should definitely be associated with postcolonial literatures elsewhere, including the revolutionary aspects of these literatures:

> It is easier for the likes of myself and other Scottish contemporary artists to talk about art, politics and culture with people from other countries.
>
> We can have straightforward conversations with African writers and writers from the West Indies and black American writers or even from Southeast Asia. You're not talking as if you've landed from Mars.
>
> You're talking about issues which are perceived as political issues: self-determination, the right of any culture to survive. These are very basic things.
>
> I would argue that the writing I do is part of this. The art form I'm engaged in is a liberation struggle. It's no accident that there is an increasing movement for self-determination in Scotland and that Scottish literature should have such a distinguishable feature to it and be vibrant as well.
>
> (quoted in 'Capturing Working Scots' Idiom')

This view is not unique to Kelman, but is also expressed by a younger Scottish writer who has been influenced by Kelman, Duncan McLean.

Again, McLean's assertion of Scottish nationalism is merged with his ideas on literature and culture. He is of the view that Scotland:

> is effectively a colony of England. Its schools and universities teach English, not Scottish, literature, and books, magazines and television are largely controlled by an English middle-class mentality. Scots seethe with resentment under the English yoke.
>
> (quoted in Downer 1996)

The sense of Scottish nationalism is certainly not dormant, and is in fact growing in some quarters. It does not merely manifest itself in the cheers of some Scotsmen whenever England loses a European or World Cup soccer match. However, Scottish nationalism as something much stronger than the support of the Scottish football team is a recent phenomenon, and can be traced to the period of Margaret Thatcher as British Prime Minister, as recounted by the reporter Ian Jack (1997: 1):

> ... in 1978, when Scotland are ejected from another World Cup, I write a piece for the Sunday Times which includes the phrase 'the great Caledonian bubble has burst'. A history professor at Glasgow University writes to the paper to say that the great Caledonian bubble will float on; nationalism has more complicated causes than football. But he is proved wrong, at least until Margaret Thatcher arrives.

Anglo-Welsh literature

We have seen the example of R.S. Thomas above, who is perhaps the most prominent Welsh nationalist writing in English. In one of his early poems 'The Old Language' (Thomas 1993: 25), he laments:

> England, what have you done to make the speech
> My fathers used a stranger at my lips,
> An offence to the ear, a shackle on the tongue ...?

However, Thomas is a paradoxical figure:

> Thomas hates the English language, yet writes his poetry in it ... His fanatical nationalism, it turns out, was a midlife growth. As a boy in Holyhead, he ... showed no inclination to learn the language, and quickly forgot the little that was taught at school ... Thomas's enemies, keen to sniff out hypocrisy, note that his much-trumpeted

Welshness did not prevent him sending his son to an English public school, Sherborne. Nor did the boy learn Welsh (though Thomas is so keen on everyone else doing so that he would not answer his parishioners if they addressed him in English).

(Carey 1996)

In fact, Thomas does not regard anyone who does not speak the Welsh language as ethnically Welsh. It can also be noted that Thomas's Welsh, which he started to learn seriously in his late twenties, suffers from being acquired late. According to some informants, it is 'stiff and academic', in contrast to the Welsh of the hill-farmers, which he admires, as it is spoken naturally, as if it bubbles 'out of them like birdsong' (Carey 1996). His Welsh can also be contrasted to his English: he speaks Welsh 'in a markedly Anglicised accent', whereas his English is spoken 'without a trace of Welsh' (Heptonstall 1997: 216). Incidentally, English was also the language he spoke with his Canadian–Irish wife at home.

Yet, in spite of the complications of his nationalistic feelings and stance, his espousal of extremist Welsh nationalism appears as plainly negative, even rabid, which, as seen earlier, led Rushdie to coin the word *nationism* to describe it. In this regard, it is understandable for Thomas to be angered when the Welsh valleys were flooded to provide Liverpool and Birmingham with drinking water. It is also understandable for him to be displeased at 'the use of the Llyn peninsula as a practice ground for RAF fighter bombers and as a rest and recreation facility for the English urban masses' (O Drisceoil 1997: 9). However, his support of violent Welsh nationalism is not always easy to understand. For example, he notoriously refused to condemn the burning of English-owned holiday cottages by Welsh extremists. When asked if he could reconcile his profession as a clergyman with his pro-extremist stance, he was rumoured to have said, 'what is the life of one English person compared to the destruction of a nation?' (Carey 1996). He is against the English who own second homes in Wales 'because their presence brought the intrusion of an unwanted alien language' (Jury 1997). As an extension of this, he believes that the Welsh should rise in armed resistance against the English. He is envious of Ireland, where, in his view, 'the English handling of the Easter 1916 uprising created martyrs who acted as the catalyst for a great nationalist movement' (Jury 1997).

Extreme nationalism was a late development in Thomas. It was a meeting with Saunders Lewis, the Welsh nationalist and writer, that changed the course of his life. Thomas met Lewis after the latter had been released from prison for subversion. The following is a description of their meeting:

Lewis broke into Welsh to which Thomas could reply only falteringly. Shame galvanised his spirit. He learned how to speak to the farm people of his parish in their own tongue. He learned how to write, though only in prose, an apparently distinguished Welsh.

(Heptonstall 1997: 215–6)

Thomas is by no means alone, among Welsh nationalists, in his late acquisition of Welsh: Gwynfor Evans, another prominent nationalist, also learnt in later in life. Although Thomas did eventually learn to write successfully in Welsh, his poetry, which he did not write in the language, 'came to be written in an exceptional English, the purity of its diction equal to the perfect measure of its prosody' (Heptonstall 1997: 216). He is aware of this anomaly, and is full of regret. For him, it feels like 'salt in the wound' that his poetry is written in English. However, he confesses that 'his grasp of Welsh lacks the necessary nuances' for him to write poetry in the language (Jury 1997).

It may be claimed that Thomas's nationalism is conspicuous in his proclamations outside his creative writing, but not really evident in his poetry. Arguably, it is present, but more subtly. According to Rushdie, Thomas's 'poems seek, by noticing, arguing, rhapsodizing, mythologizing, to write the nation to fierce, lyrical being' (Rushdie 1997b: 22). It is difficult, to Rushdie, for writers 'to deny the lure of the nation, its tides in our blood' (1997b: 22). However, 'In the best writing, ... a map of a nation will also turn out to be a map of the world' (1997b: 24), which is why the nationalism in much of Thomas's poetry can only be detected with some discrimination. What Rushdie describes as Thomas's 'nationism' is overtly presented in only a few of his poems, of which 'The Old Language', which was partly quoted above, is an example. However, it is very clear in many of his extra-poetic proclamations.

Use of dialects and linguistic violence

Although the writers may use English, one of the ways they assert their sense of nationalism is through the use of dialects of English not found in England itself. The use of dialect to assert nationalism varies in the non-English states. In a recent anthology of poetry from Wales, for example, it has been noted that only two of the poets use Anglo-Welsh dialects in their writing (Firchow 1995: 591). However, there is a clear tendency to use dialect for the expression of a national identity in the case of recent fiction from Scotland. Sometimes, this is done through what can be described as *linguistic violence*, as in the case of James Kelman and Irvine Welsh.

James Kelman

One of Kelman's novels *How Late It Was, How Late* (1994) has been described as 'expletive-filled' and 'attracted reviews that spluttered with sanctimonious wrath' (Huggan 1997: 416). One of these reviews was written in *The Times* by Simon Jenkins, who 'compared reading the novel to being waylaid in a railway carriage by a Glaswegian drunk' (Jaggi 1998). According to Jenkins, who was speaking from personal experience, the Glaswegian drunkard, who reminded him so much of Kelman, and whom he describes as 'an ambassador of that city', 'requested money with menaces, swore and eventually relieved himself into the seat' (cited by Wood 1994: 9). The following extract is quite typical of Kelman's novel (1998: 171) as a whole:

> But it couldnay get worse than this. He was really fuckt now. This was the dregs; he was at it. He had fucking reached it now man the fucking dregs man the pits, the fucking black fucking limboland, purgatory; that's what it was like, purgatory, where all ye can do is think. Think. That's all ye can do. Ye just fucking think about what ye've done and what ye've no fucking done; ye cannay look at nothing ye cannay see nothing it's just a total fucking disaster area, yer mind, yer fucking memories, a disaster area. Ye wonder about these things. How come it happened to you and nay other cunt? He wasnay ordinary, that's the thing man, Sammy, he wasnay ordinary, cause if he was fucking ordinary it wouldnay be fucking happening. That's how ye've got to look at yer life, what ye did that made ye different. And it's all fucking bastard fucking flukes man fucking coincidences. Even going blind. Although it didnay just HAPPEN I mean it didnay just HAPPEN; fucking spontaneous, it wasnay spontaneous, it was these bastard sodjers, it was them, stupit fucking fuckpig bastards.

In an extract of one hundred and ninety words, the root word 'fuck' appears seventeen times, which means that it makes its appearance in every eleven words, which is probably reflective of the novel as a whole. If the words 'bastard' (thrice in the extract) and 'cunt' (once) are added, scatalogical words or root words appear once in every ten words, which is very frequent indeed. Stylistically, these words either have the effect of being incantatory, or, as is more likely the case, become monotonous after a while.

The negative reaction to Kelman's novel is thus not entirely surprising. Simon Jenkins called Kelman an 'illiterate savage'. However, to the surprise of some of his critics (including, presumably, Jenkins himself), there is a deeper side to Kelman. He has, for example, actually read 'the European masters to whom he is compared – Beckett, Kafka, Joyce, Chekhov, Zola' (Jaggi 1998). *How Late It Was, How Late* won the Booker Prize in 1994. Jenkins denounced the award to Kelman and deprecated the quality of the novel by describing it as an example of 'literary vandalism'; one of the judges for that year, Rabbi Julia Neuberger, described the book as 'crap' and 'not publicly accessible' (Jaggi 1998). During his acceptance speech, Kelman denounced the English as colonialists. The Irish author Roddy Doyle also uses dialect with f-words in his novel *Paddy Clark Ha Ha Ha*, which won the Booker the year before, but he is not as interested as Kelman in politicising the issue of language use.

Irvine Welsh

Another novelist with the same tendency is Irvine Welsh, whose language in his novels has been described as 'scabrous' and 'foul-mouthed' (Downer 1996). Although he used the f-word only sixty-one times in his first work for television (Cosgrove 1997: 22) – a far cry from Kelman's novel, which was estimated to have contained 'about 4,000 f-words' (Ellison 1994: 1) – it must be remembered that television is a more conservative linguistic medium than the contemporary Scottish novel. There are certainly many more f-words in Irvine Welsh's cult novel *Trainspotting* (1993):

> Now the doorbell's going. Fuckin hell. That bastard shite-arsed fuck-up of a landlord: Baxter's son. Auld Baxter, god rest the diddy cunt's soul, never bothered aboot the rent cheque. Senile auld wanker.
>
> (Welsh 1996: 86)

However, in the novel as a whole, Welsh uses scatological words and expressions slightly more sparingly than Kelman, which is not saying much, as they certainly appear much more frequently than in the average novel in English.

Here is a description of the language used in Welsh's work:

> A gang of Edinburgh men — heroin addicts, boozers, streetfighters, football hooligans, sometimes all four at once — make an anarchic, episodic and brutal passage through this novel.
>
> They speak their own language, which is slangy, filthy and unwriteable. But since the novel is narrated by various members of this gang, this language must be written down. It is forced to become a "literary" language, the language of fictional narration ...
>
> (Wood 1996: C34)

Whatever it is, there is no question that there is an attempt to represent a Scottish dialect of English in his novel, even if, with Kelman's extra-literary pronouncements in mind, Welsh's general sense of Scottish nationalism is relatively less palpable. Although the main character of *Trainspotting* says that 'Ah've never felt British, because ah'm not. It's ugly and artificial', he also says that:

> Ah've never really felt Scottish either, though. Scotland the brave, ma arse; Scotland the shitein cunt. We'd throttle the life oot ay each other fir the privilege ay rimmin some English aristocrat's piles.
>
> (Welsh 1996: 228)

It is clear that being 'Scottish' is tantamount to being subservient to the English. The romanticised version of Scotland associated with kilts and bagpipes has no place in *Trainspotting*. There is an anarchic thrust in the novel which makes it anti-colonial, even if its sense of Scottishness does not call out for attention on the surface: 'Ah've never felt a fuckin thing aboot countries, other than total disgust' (Welsh 1996: 228). Nevertheless, going to London in the novel is still viewed in terms of an 'exile'.

There is one aspect of Welsh's language use that is quite different from that of Kelman's. It has been noted that while 'Kelman's characters swear in a writerly sort of way', 'Welsh's voices are the ones you would hear on the Muirhouse bus or at Easter Road when Hibs are losing' (McKay 1996). It is therefore less easy to understand, as it is closer to the spoken dialect, and even the *Guardian* reviewer Tom Shields (1996: 27) confesses that he 'needs a glossary to keep up'. However, the making of Welsh's novel into a film has helped to reverse the situation, and it is probably the case today that Welsh's language in the novel is understood better than the language of Kelman's novel.

The f-word and anti-colonialism: an Australian digression

The 'subversive' language of Kelman and Welsh can be described as anti-colonial. But what is so anti-colonial about the f-word? In order to answer that question in wider perspective, let us look at how its use was perceived in relation to a noteworthy incident in Australian theatre. In 1968, the play *Norm and Ahmed* by Alex Buzo was premiered. The performance included the f-word, and, as a result, several members of its cast were arrested. This incident must be viewed within the wider context of the use of what was regarded as 'obscene' language in

Australian literature. The Australian poet John Tranter (1996) notes, for example, that 'No poet in Australia in the late Fifties and early Sixties could get a poem published in any magazine if the editor thought that it might in any way give moral offence to the average person'. Tranter views this moral squeamishness in the use of language in Australian literature in terms of Australia's 'long and miserable tradition of subservience to authority: the ghost of our convict past'.

With regard to *Norm and Ahmed*, the Australian theatre scholars Helen Gilbert and Joanne Tompkins (1996) have no doubt about the f-word in the play as an emblem of anti-colonialism (or the powerful expression of postcolonial anti-British sentiments). Linguistically, they view its use in the play as a potent indication of its wider usage in Australian English *vis-à-vis* what is regarded as 'standard' British English. This was how they perceive its presence in the play:

> Whether or not this language [as it is used in the play] was a serious attempt to address British control over Australian affairs, it was *interpreted* as a nationalist move by which Australia declared a metaphoric independence: the ensuing furore that the arrests created assisted in the easing of Australia's censorship rules. *Norm and Ahmed*, together with many other Australian plays of the 1960s and 1970s, established as 'legitimate' on local stages the Australian colloquial and metaphoric 'dialect' of English that incorporates particular idiomatic expressions and rhyming slang.
>
> (Gilbert and Tompkins 1996: 165–6)

In this light, the f-word is seen as an emblem of a more extensive dialectal usage and as significant in the conflict with the colonial inheritance. The latter is an important consideration in the interpretation of recent Scottish fiction in terms of anti-colonial literature. Gilbert and Tompkins have also made another important point: that the dialect may be 'metaphorical', which is relevant for the analysis of Kelman, who may not give a faithful representation of any actual spoken Scottish dialect. Besides, the faithful representation of dialects in literature is always difficult, and most dialectal representations may after all be, to a degree, metaphorical.

The f-word and anti-colonialism: back to Kelman

Kelman nonchalantly asserts that the f-word is a regular part of his own language and dialect, and innocently claims that although it is frequently used in his childhood and teens, he did not know what it was supposed to mean (or what its 'standard' meaning was) until much later. Kelman 'claims only to have been aware of the original meaning of the word "fuck" when he was in his twenties: hitherto, the word had had a hundred other meanings, a thousand different uses' (Bell 1994: 16). As in the Australian case above, Kelman's use of the f-word is emblematic of his attempt to include a non-standard dialect in his work. In this light, the language used in his work has been regarded as 'real speech, speech that only becomes controversial in the artificial environment of "official" English' (Bell 1994: 16). A letter writer in the *Observer* has also pointed out that Kelman 'and his characters are in mourning for the slow death since the 18th century of their native language: Lowland Scots', and because of the lack of 'a mature language for the expression of feelings he resorts to the poor substitute of debased English' (McLellan 1994: 28). However, so different is Kelman's English from the 'official' English that we are familiar with, that a Booker manager declared that the novel 'wasn't even written in English' (Kelman 1998: 24).

If the English refuse to accept Kelman's wide-ranging polysemous usage of the f-word – which is more widely emblematic of his own regionally based language and is abundantly exemplified in his works – then his attitude to their refusal could be described as confrontational. In this regard, Kelman blatantly repudiates the English's view of what their language should be. The prominence of the award of the Booker Prize to Kelman may also have a transformative effect on British culture, or, as is more likely, the novel confirms a transformation which has already occurred within British society, but which is not liked in some quarters. After Kelman won the award, a report by David Harrison in the *Observer* prefaced itself with the following:

> WARNING: This article contains words that some readers may find offensive, although some will find them less offensive than they did a few years ago. And some will not find them offensive at all. A few may even like them.
>
> (Harrison 1994: 9)

To Harrison, *How Late It Was, How Late* 'makes the expletive almost defunct, but not deleted', and 'confirmed what many language purists had suspected – swearing has become so common that we may have to invent new expletives in order to shock'. Harrison even coins a new word, *Kelmanism*, in order to encapsulate a new transformation that, according to him, has occurred in British popular culture:

The Kelman-word now appears brazenly on T-shirts. Comics such as Viz and Smut are studded with Kelmanisms and references to illegitimacy. The first dozen words in the film Four Weddings and a Funeral – hailed as the best British film for years – are loud Kelmanisms.

Harrison also notes that such 'Kelmanisms' were becoming more widespread in the newspapers in 1993:

> The *Independent* and its Sunday sister have used the Kelman-word 232 times in the past year, up from a modest eight in the restrained days of 1988. The *Guardian* has done so 227 times in the past 12 months. The *Observer* had 49 examples last year.

The tabloids, however, are sensitive to their readers' feelings, and hardly ever use f-words, although 'they are partial to asterisks, stars and exclamation marks that leave little to the imagination' (Harrison 1994: 9).

The f-word, it has also been argued, has a long historical relationship with Scottish culture and literature. Thus, Kelman puts himself, at least as he probably wants to see himself, as a representative of Scottish literary tradition, under which, in Wood's words (1994: 9), 'he shelters so noisily', and this allows him to astringently pit himself against the English literary tradition:

> Like most debates about language and ideology, there is a specifically Scottish dimension to the story of fuck. The word has a long and honourable literary history in Scotland, appearing in the work of the medieval poets Henryson and Dunbar, and developing through the renaissance to appear across many areas of literature and society. Robert Burns also found it a useful linguistic expression – using it sparingly in his poetry but promiscuously in his private life.
>
> In modern Scotland, the word fuck is an invasive part of the popular vernacular, punctuating everyday conversation and multiplying in importance as it goes. It figures in whole swathes of comedy and most importantly of all is a crucial part of the grainy realism of contemporary fiction. From the bleak modernism of James Kelman's novels to the acidic fantasies of Irvine Welsh, the word fuck – and its ovular equivalent, cunt – are used not simply to reflect the cadences of working-class life, but to mark out the power of a language that is inarticulate yet profound.
>
> (Cosgrove 1998)

Of course, it may be regarded as a caricature of the situation to say that Kelman's influence on the younger nationalist Scottish writers is centred on the f-word. It may also be counter-argued that the f-word is also part of Englishness: after all, wasn't it Philip Larkin, that 'key figure in the concept of Englishness in modern literature', 'who made the word "fuck" fully canonical' (Crawford 1992: 273, 275)? If too much can be made of the f-word and Scottish nationalism, and, more specifically, its representativeness in Kelman's language, so can too little be made of it. Whatever it is, there is something in the language of Kelman's fiction that creates an impact on younger Scottish writers. What is regarded as obscene language in his novels is, in effect, part and parcel of his influence, and should be emblematically viewed in terms of the wider usage of dialect or the representation of Scottish culture. It can be noted that even in Larkin's case, the use of 'four-letter words that play off against gentilities can be seen as [his] equivalent of dialect' (Crawford 1992: 276, citing Blake Morrison). The impact of Kelman's writing with regard to dialect and the representation of Scottish culture has been described by the writer Duncan McLean:

> As soon as I came across him, I thought, 'This is it.' He was writing about a Scotland I recognised using a language I recognised.
>
> (cited by Wroe 1997: 12)

The anti-colonial attitude of Kelman towards England, the English, and English culture has been seen earlier. This attitude is closely tied up to the survival of his language and culture: 'My culture and my language have the right to exist, and no one has the authority to dismiss that right' (quoted in Jaggi 1998). The writer A.L. Kennedy elaborates (1996: 19):

> We have served England's crown, we have died for England's empire, we have seen our Gaels subjected to genocide in the 18th century, and our urban poor to needless and fatal poverty. For generations, we have been told that we are awkwardly different and expendable. We had to find this funny and fascinating, or go insane.

One of the ways to rebel against the colonial masters is to resort to language, and the language of literature in particular:

> Having been drowned out by other cultures for so long, we now intend to be heard. Having been told that our languages, dialects

and accents are wrong and intrinsically subversive, we take delight in subverting.

(Kennedy 1996: 19)

It is in this respect that Andrew Neil (1998: 11) has noted (albeit negatively) that the 'foul-mouthed, anti-English rant of an Edinburgh heroin crackhead in *Trainspotting* has been made into Scotland's Gettysburg Address by fashionable bletherers.'

Suppression of the Celtic languages

Looking backwards, one of the major effects of the conquest of Wales, Scotland and Ireland and their continued colonisation over the centuries, was the suppression of the Celtic languages. The linguistic suppression was also seen in other parts of the British Isles. Some of these Celtic languages, such as Manx and Cornish – the latter was spoken within England itself in Cornwall – have become extinct, although there have been attempts to revive Cornish, which now has around 2,000 speakers. Irish Gaelic has only about half a million speakers in Ireland, and there is a corresponding number of Welsh speakers in Wales. Scotland has fewer than 80,000 speakers of Scottish Gaelic.

Among the reasons for the suppression of the Celtic languages was their deficiency, it was claimed, when compared with English. As a corollary, it has been argued that the speakers of Celtic languages can improve themselves materially or professionally if they abandoned their languages and used English. On the surface at least, such sentiments did seem to be positive, as they attempted to 'improve' the well-being of people, although the means by which this could be done – by 'rescuing them from their own language' – does seem dubious. Here, for example, is the 1866 editorial in *The Times*, which questioned Matthew Arnold's advocacy of the study of Welsh:

> The Welsh language is the curse of Wales. Its prevalence and the ignorance of English have excluded, and even now exclude, the Welsh people from the civilization, the improvement, and the material prosperity of their English neighbours ... [T]he Welsh have remained in Wales, unable to mix with their fellow-subjects, shut out from all literature except what is translated into their own language and incapable of progress ... Their antiquated and semi-barbarous language, in short, shrouds them in darkness. If Wales and the Welsh are ever thoroughly to share in the material

prosperity, and, in spite of Mr. Arnold, we will add the culture and morality, of England, they must forget their isolated language, and learn to speak English, and nothing else.

(cited in Dawson and Pfordresher 1979: 161–2)

Survival of the Celtic languages

In spite of their small number of speakers when compared with English, literatures in the Celtic languages continue to be written, even in the least spoken of the three surviving Celtic languages in the British Isles today, Scottish Gaelic. They need to be mentioned here, lest the impression is created that literatures in these languages have completely succumbed to the onslaught of English.

Scottish Gaelic

Among the important writers in Scottish Gaelic this century are the poet Sorley Maclean and the novelist Iain Crichton Smith. They are regarded as major twentieth-century writers in the language. Gaelic literature in Scotland has a strong relationship with nationalism, and Maclean's poetry is believed to have a significant part to play in it. It has been argued, for example, that as a result of Maclean's 'poetry more than to anything else', 'Gaelic remains central in the perception of Scottish culture shared by youthful generations' (Calder and Wilson 1996: 11). However, Scottish Gaelic, with fewer than 80,000 speakers, is a language under threat.

To be fair, Scottish Gaelic is not the only indigenous language. Scots, which has more speakers, and is not a Gaelic language, has also made a strong claim to being a native language of Scotland. Indeed, Scots has been used more often for the linguistic expression of Scottish nationalism than Scottish Gaelic, with the use of the language by James Kelman, during the presentation ceremony for the award of the Booker Prize to him in 1994, being a recent example. However, Scots is often treated as a dialect or even a variety of English (Carter and McRae 1997: 532–3), and it had a historical relationship with the English spoken in Northern England. The use of Scots in literature, as in the case of Kelman and Welsh discussed above, in fact provides interesting examples of how varieties or dialects of English can be used in literary works (for further examples, see Carter and McRae 1997: 204–7, 379–80, 532–4, 536–7).

Welsh

Perhaps the most visible literature written in a Celtic language today is found in Wales, as Welsh is more of a living literary language in the British Isles today than the other Celtic languages. A contributory factor here is the number of its speakers. Welsh is the mother tongue of about a fifth of the population of Wales. As such, it certainly has more speakers, as noted above, than Scottish Gaelic in Scotland (although there are faint hopes that the granting of more autonomy to Scotland may change that). In this regard, R.S. Thomas proudly commented that 'Language is where the Welsh outshine the Irish and the Scots' and that ' "We are superior" ' in the use of Welsh when compared with the Scots and Irish (quoted by Jury 1997). Perhaps, unlike Scotland, Wales does not also have a competing English-based dialect making a strong claim to being the language of nationalism.

However, the view that Welsh is a living language has been questioned. It may be a literary language, but whether it is a healthy living language like English or French is a different matter. It has been noted, for instance, that even though it is claimed that '18 per cent of the Welsh speak the language ... 82 per cent do not speak it at all' (Rogers 1997: 31). It is further noted, even though it is 'a fact ... hard to believe', 'that twice as many people speak Breton [the Celtic language spoken in France] as its sister language Welsh' (Rogers 1997: 31).

With the ideas of 'purity' discussed in the previous chapter in mind, it may also be mentioned here, that during the sixteenth century, the Welsh were regarded as the descendants of the original pre-Roman population of the British Isles. The Tudor dynasty in fact legitimised itself as the ruling dynasty in Britain by appealing to their remote Welsh ancestry. However, this did not do much to enhance the status of the Welsh people and the Welsh language over the centuries, although the idea of purity, in terms of both ethnicity and language, seems to have survived among Welsh nationalists. R.S. Thomas, for example, laments that 'The ties between the Welsh and the English are too many': 'The people inter-marry, they barely notice they are crossing the river Severn – or Hafren in Welsh' (quoted by Jury 1997).

Irish

The Irish are usually happy if writers write in Gaelic in general, even in Scots Gaelic. However, this does not mean that the situation with Irish Gaelic in Ireland itself is completely rosy. Although literature in the language continues to be written, songs (including popular songs) continue to be sung in it and Irish is the first official language of Ireland, some doubts on the staying power of the language have been expressed. Like the situation in Wales and Scotland, many Irish writers prefer to write in English. Yeats and Joyce have been mentioned above; they wrote in English so well that they give further credence to the observation that 'the English gave us their language and we gave them literature.' Even when the mother tongue of the writer was Irish, some of them preferred to write in English, as in the case of Flann O'Brien, who chose to write most of his novels in English.

On a lighter note, the following is a short account of the experience of two linguists when they were in Ireland. The anecdote refers to a single occasion, but it does appear to be reflective of the situation of Irish in Ireland today:

> Late one night, eminent linguist Joshua Fishman and a colleague were crossing the lobby of their Dublin hotel when the cleaner leaned on his mop and exclaimed 'God love you. Two sons of Ireland speaking the language of their fathers.' Fishman and Robert Cooper, who had just flown from Tel Aviv, paused from speaking Yiddish, thanked the old man, and went on to the bar.
>
> (Maher 1998)

On a more serious note, it has been argued by Maher (quite contrary to the anecdote he presented above) that while 'fewer primary school students [in Ireland] study Irish intensively in bilingual programs, more children study Irish as a school subject over a longer period (i.e. to 18 years)'. He believes that there is a resurgence of the language via the educational system, as 'the higher percentage [of Irish speakers] within younger age groups reflects the initial impact of revival strategies'. However the continued survival of the language, and the role educational institutions play in ensuring its survival, have been put into serious question by some specialists in Gaelic. The following, for example, is the view of Shane Gallagher (1998: 15):

> Irish Gaelic is in grave danger of becoming extinct despite what any politician or educationist says. That is why it is on the UN list of endangered languages. Irish education policy towards the language has systematically failed the people of Ireland for the past 75 years. It certainly failed me. This is because the policy has been created by people who clearly have had no understanding of the nature of language.

Pattern seen in other postcolonial literatures

The pattern seen here is not unique to Britain, but, in varying degrees, is also seen in some of the lands colonised by Britain (although, admittedly, there may be more positive patterns for certain languages):

- First, there was British conquest or occupation
- The native language of the colony was then suppressed, or at best became less relevant. In the case of Welsh for example, its unconditional use in the law courts was only allowed in 1967, with the passing of the Welsh Language Act.
- The native language, if it did not have a written script and a literary tradition to back it up, gradually had fewer speakers, and may eventually become extinct. Relatively speaking, this was the case with Cornish, which became extinct more than two hundred years ago, and which did not have as strong a writing tradition as the major surviving Celtic languages today
- On a more universal scale, the colonial situation in Britain was repeated elsewhere, as eulogized in the following quotation from an anonymous article published in the middle of the nineteenth century:

> The barbarism of Australia, the heathen institutions and worn-out languages of India, the superannuated hieroglyphs of China, and the rude utterances of important parts of Africa and of numberless islands in the Eastern seas, are fast giving way to the institutions and the languages of our race.
>
>   ('Our Language Destined to be Universal', 1855: 311)

Extent of applicability to other postcolonial literatures

One broad similarity, however, between what is now increasingly described as the British states colonised by England and the former British colonies (except, to an extent, the United States) is the treatment meted out to their literatures in English. Their literatures, if taught at all, were either subsumed under English literature or they were simply ignored. It is only in recent years that this has changed. Even then, the similarity ends there, as there are comparative differences between them. Scottish, Welsh and Irish literatures in English are often subsumed under English literature, whereas the former colonies' literatures are more often ignored.

There are further problems if the situation in the other nations of the British Isles is faithfully applied to other postcolonial literatures. Here are some of the difficulties, with specific reference to the literature of Ireland:

> According to a current and – it seems to me – naive emphasis in Irish studies, we are to think of Ireland as a postcolonial country and bring to bear upon it the vocabularies of Frantz Fanon, Edward Said, Homi Bhabha, Fredric Jameson, Chinua Achebe, and other political thinkers. The fact that those vocabularies were designed to deal with historical and political conditions in Africa, India, Algeria, and the Middle East rather than in Ireland is not allowed to count.
>
> Yet England has not been an imperial force in Ireland in the way that it was in India; by the same token, the historical relations between England and Ireland are quite different from those between Belgium and the Congo. To treat the situations intellectually as one and the same is flagrant distortion.
>
> (Donoghue 1997)

However, the extent of the similarities should not be under-emphasised either. In a fine book-length discussion of the devolution of Scottish literature and other literatures in English, Robert Crawford points out that Scottish literature 'offers the longest continuing example of a substantial body of literature produced by a culture pressurized by the threat of English cultural domination' (Crawford 1992: 8). Irish and Welsh literatures also have long histories of being pressurised by English cultural domination. Their literatures can thus be associated with many of the problems in the other literatures to be discussed later in the book.

3 Anglo-Saxon transplantations

The pattern noted at the end of the previous chapter was clearly seen in the United States. After British occupation, many of the Native American languages were suppressed, and some eventually became extinct. Another linguistic effect of British colonialism was on English itself. In the United States, there was the belief that American varieties of English were of lower prestige than some varieties spoken in England, or that they were degraded versions of English. A similarly negative attitude was displayed towards American literature. In a wider context, comparable attitudes towards language and literature were seen in the other white settler colonies, such as Australia, Canada and New Zealand.

Clearly, a more positive image of their language and literature was needed. It was America that led the way by increasing the prestige of its language and literature during the course of the twentieth century, and, as such, it will form the focus of the discussion in the early part of this chapter. In the later decades of the twentieth century, the growth in the prestige of the varieties of English and literatures of the other settler colonies followed the American example. Their growth eventually had an effect on, or set the example for, the other varieties of English and literatures in the language across the globe. America is also of interest because, in spite of its anti-colonial and postcolonial credentials, it is the country which is often described today as colonial, or as displaying colonial attitudes towards other countries in the world.

In this chapter, there will also be a brief discussion of a linguistic thread that runs through the literatures of the white settler colonies. When compared with the other former British colonies, there is a stronger desire in the settler colonies, in spite of some notable exceptions, to preserve the English language as it is and not to make radical changes to it. In order to see more striking linguistic experimentations, usually influenced by other languages, one has to turn to the minority authors, or authors who are not of Anglo-Saxon origin. Some of the authors will be discussed in this chapter, and others, such as Sandra Cisneros from America, Patricia Grace from New Zealand and Essop Patel from South Africa, will be discussed in later chapters.

American national identity via literature and language

After independence from Britain, there was a need for American writers and Americans in general to express or assert their American identity. One way to do this was through language. The problem of course, is that the Americans, like the British, use English. In fact, at an earlier stage in post-independent America, it was believed that the standard to attain was based on what was believed to be the standard in British English. For example, Benjamin Franklin told the Scottish philosopher David Hume that 'the best British English would always be the American standard' (cited by Bridgman 1966: 40), and in early nineteenth-century America Americanisms continued to be viewed in terms of a 'barbarous phraseology'. Thus, the idea of a British-based standard made the attempt to create a separate identity more problematic.

Noah Webster and the 'American' language

As a counter-thrust to the creation of a British-based standard, it was suggested that one way to develop a separate American identity was to allow the language to naturally develop in such a way that it became a different language in its own right. This was the view of the American lexicographer Noah Webster, as expressed, for example, in his *Dissertations on the English Language*, published in 1789. In the *Dissertations*, Webster proclaimed that American English would eventually emerge as a language that was distinct from English. Webster was proved wrong: American English did not develop into another language in the way Italian and French did from Latin. However, Webster had an influential supporter in the twentieth century in the person of H.L. Mencken, who believed that a separate language called 'American', which was quite distinct from English, had actually developed.

It should also be noted that Webster's dictionary, published in 1828, was collated with the belief that the words should be based on spoken language. However, the dictionary was initially criticised for its 'Americanism' and unusual spelling. Forty-five years before the dictionary, Webster had compiled the *American Spelling Book*, which is now regarded as one of the critical texts in the development of American English orthography. Among the spelling reforms he initiated were the dropping of the letter 'u' in the 'ou' sequence in words such as 'honour' and 'labour', which are now spelt 'honor' and 'labor' in texts published in the United States.

Webster can be regarded as an American nationalist who believed that the culture of the United States should not be neglected in education, including English language education. Webster's importance in the American postcolonial search for a national identity which is distinct from that of their past masters in England should not be underestimated. V.P. Bynack (1984: 99–100) has correctly described him as 'one of the first proponents of the idea of a unified national culture after the revolution'. It is significant that Webster thought that language should play a crucial role in cementing together the American nation, and creating for it its national identity.

Walt Whitman

The fact that American English did not evolve into a language that was distinct from British English did not prevent American writers from desiring to express their nationalism through the use of what they thought were distinctive features of American English, even if they did not have a wholly distinct language to express it with. One of the writers was Whitman, who claimed that there were:

> ten thousand idiomatic native words ..., out of which vast numbers could be used by American writers, with meaning and effect – words that would be welcomed by the nation, being of the national blood – words that would give that taste of identity and locality which is so dear in literature
>
> (cited in Chamberlin 1993: 88).

Whitman was responsible for introducing a colloquial and matter-of-fact style to poetry, which, at one time, was taken to be part of the American contribution to literature in English. Charles Eliot Norton (1855), for example, describes *Leaves of Grass* (1855) in terms of a 'mixture of Yankee transcendentalism and New York rowdyism'. Whitman ([1855] 1982b: 1166) writes that American English is not 'an abstract construction of the learned, or of dictionary makers, but is something arising out of the work needs, ties, joys, affections, tastes, of long generations of humanity, and has its basis broad and low, close to the ground'. More generally, Whitman has been described as 'the first American poet whose work carries, however crudely at times, the whole sense of America and of being an American' (Moore 1969: xii).

However, quite apart from the spirit in which Whitman's poems were written, it is difficult to linguistically pinpoint what exactly is 'American' about his poetry. The following lines from *Leaves of Grass* (Whitman [1855] 1982a: 174) serve as an illustration:

> I HEAR America singing, the varied carols I hear;
> Those of mechanics – each one singing his, as it should be, blithe
>   and strong;
> The carpenter singing his, as he measures his plank or beam,
> The mason singing his, as he makes ready for work, or leaves off
>   work;
> The boatman singing what belongs to him in his boat – the deckhand
>   singing on the steamboat deck;

A British poet might very well have used the language found in the above, or in most of the other poems in the volume.

The 'American' quality of *Leaves of Grass* has been an issue in the criticism of the poem. Any considered opinion of the collection will almost certainly arrive at the conclusion that, in linguistic terms, it is not as substantial as the casual reader thinks it is, or as Whitman himself wanted it to be (see Coy 1936). Mencken (1974: 81) complains that 'more than half his innovations were simply borrowings from finishing-school French, with a few examples of Spanish and Italian added for good measure'.

Literary genres and the postcolonial assertion of nationalism

In reflecting on what Whitman tries to do in his poetry, however, one must note the belief that there is a relative generic difference between poetry and prose or drama in the use of the language actually spoken by a particular community. Grahame Johnston (1967: 26) has summed up the prevalent view on this issue when he says that 'It has often been noted by critics that the diction of modern poetry in English is international, so that it would be hard to tell an unsigned lyric by an Australian or an American from one by an Englishman or a New Zealander'. A similar disjunction is seen when moving from Australian literature, which is the focus of Johnston's comment, to India, where Parthasarathy (1976: 7) notes that Indian poets have not been able to 'Indianize' English as successfully as novelists such as Raja Rao and G.V. Desani. Moving to the Caribbean, varieties of the colloquial language spoken in the Caribbean are more persistently present in Derek Walcott's plays when compared with his poetry. Likewise, the use of colloquial English does seem to be less prominent in Singapore poetry in English, when compared with fictional prose (Talib 1999: 123–4).

The significance of Mark Twain

Mark Twain (pseudonym of Samuel Langhorne Clemens), aided by this generic advantage, goes much further than Whitman in the use of a distinctive variety of American English. Twain can be regarded as a significant figure in the effective postcolonial dissociation of literary English from its mother country. Although Twain was not the first writer who attempted to use American dialects in his work (see Simpson 1986: 101–18), no one before him used them as persistently, as effectively and with as much aesthetic success as he did in *Huckleberry Finn* ([1874] 1943). With this novel, according to Grahame Johnston (1967: 22), 'American writing ceased to be colonial because it at last asserted the strength, honesty and vigour of the vernacular'.

Twain claims in the explanatory note to the novel ([1874] 1943: 183) that:

> … a number of dialects are used, to wit: the Missouri Negro dialect; the extremest form of the backwoods South-Western dialect; the ordinary 'Pike-Country' dialect; and four modified varieties of this last. The shadings have not been done in a haphazard fashion, or by guesswork; but painstakingly, and with the trustworthy guidance and support of personal familiarity with these several forms of speech.

Whether Twain was successful in the exact recreation of the above dialects of American English is a moot point, and there is always the expected difference between the aesthetic representations of languages and dialects and their counterparts in the real world. Whatever it is, there is no doubt that Twain made a conscious attempt to use language that was different from the language usually associated with the writing of literature in English, which at that time was dominated by British models. His use of language in the novel represents certain varieties of English that can only be found in the United States. The following is quite typical of the language used in the novel as a whole:

> I CREPT to their doors and listened; they was snoring. So I tiptoed along, and got down stairs all right. There warn't a sound anywheres. I peeped through a crack of the dining-room door, and see the men

that was watching the corpse all sound asleep on their chairs. The door was open into the parlor, where the corpse was laying, and there was a candle in both rooms. I passed along, and the parlor door was open; but I see there warn't nobody in there but the remainders of Peter; so I shoved on by; but the front door was locked, and the key wasn't there.

(1943: 338)

There are some features in the above extract that are quite distinctive to Huck's language in the novel, which according to Twain, in the explanatory note to the novel quoted earlier, is representative of a dialect of English spoken in the Mississippi. Among the distinctive features are the lack of plural concord in the verbs being used: 'they was snoring', and 'the men that was watching'; the use of the negative polar verb 'warn't' instead of 'wasn't'; the use of double negatives: 'there warn't nobody in there'; and the use of the lexical item 'anywheres', which is the adverbial anywhere with an 's' added at the end.

Some of the peculiarities of the use of language in *Huckleberry Finn* may be found in some dialects of British English, but unlike Whitman's poetry, it is improbable that a British writer could have produced the language found in the above, or elsewhere in the novel. The unlikely exception would be a British writer who had lived in the region of the United States where the dialect was supposed to have been taken from. Although some British film actors are very good in their imitation of American accents, British creative writers who engage in the sustained recreation of varieties of American English in an extended work of literature, such as Martin Amis in his novel *Night Train*, seem to be much less common.

One judgment that is frequently encountered in critics' assessment of the significance of Twain's *Huckleberry Finn* is that it is quintessentially American. The novel has been described as 'that most American book' by Robert Weisbuch (1986: 130), and, in the most famous judgment of the novel from another novelist, Hemingway (1954: 29) pronounces that:

All modern American literature comes from one book by Mark Twain called *Huckleberry Finn* … it's the best book we've had. All American writing comes from that. There was nothing before. There has been nothing as good since.

Hemingway (1954: 28) indicates the postcolonial significance of Twain's work by singling him out from older American authors such as 'Emerson,

Hawthorne and Whittier and Company', who 'wrote like exiled English colonials from an England of which they were never a part to a newer England that they were making'. As an important part of the Americanness of the novel has to do with its use of language, Twain's book appears to be a clear illustration of McLuhan's view (1962: 218) that 'there cannot be nationalism where there has not first been an experience of a vernacular in printed form'.

Within the context of the aftermath of British imperialism, Twain's use of language in *Huckleberry Finn* has an important part to play in making it the first significant postcolonial literary work in English. What Twain does is to effect a triumphant linguistic revolt from the belief 'that the mark of the truly literary product was a grandiosity and elegance not to be found in the common speech' (Trilling 1951: 117). By doing this, he manages 'to liberate himself from the grip of an approved literary style that bore no relation to living American speech' and, in effect, to 'exorcise European culture' from his art (Podhoretz 1959). T.S. Eliot makes an assessment of the postcolonial linguistic importance of Twain's book when he expresses the view, as summarised by Alex Zwerdling (1998: 310), that 'The American writer here is the forerunner, his language not subject to an English imprimatur'. Defiantly going against the denigration of American dialects by Americans themselves, Twain persistently uses the 'barbarous phraseology' of some American dialects in an extended narrative with a vengeance, and successfully turns the text written in them into a popular and influential work of art.

Twain's influence on later postcolonial writers should not be underestimated, even if, in some ways, he is not a representative figure. Although influential on later American writers, especially in bringing about the sense of linguistic liberation from English literary modes of expression, American authors were in a sense divided between what has been described as the 'redskins' and 'palefaces' (Rahv 1939). The latter (which comes from the native American term for white men) are interested in maintaining the American connection to Europe and England, whereas the former are directed towards severing the link.

It is to the 'redskins', of which Twain is a towering figure, that one must look when one searches for the precursors or earliest exemplars of postcolonial literatures in English. As the Caribbean novelist George Lamming (1992: 29) has reminded us, 'the West Indian novel, particularly in the aspect of idiom, cannot be understood unless you take a good look at the American nineteenth century, a good look at Melville, Whitman and Mark Twain'. Melville's importance can be mentioned in passing here, as he is also interested, to a certain extent, in liberating the language from the influence of British English, and there are, arguably, parallels in some aspects of his language with the language of postcolonial authors such as Achebe (Buell 1992: 411). Melville has also been related to postcolonialism more generally (Sanborn 1998). However, Twain accomplishes the task of liberating the language more forcefully and more comprehensively in *Huckleberry Finn* than Melville in any of his works. Lamming puts the focus on Twain when he says that West Indian authors have not tried 'to play at being the Eliots and Henry Jameses of the West Indies', but have instead moved 'nearer to Mark Twain' (1992: 38).

Twain is not a representative figure in another sense. Although his work can be described as embodying the height of American postcolonial literature, it came about at the moment that America itself was beginning to turn into a colonial power in its own right. To his credit, and, in an affirmation of his role as postcolonial author, Twain was a critic of aspects of early American imperialism, such as its expansionist designs on the Philippines. It is to this other side of the United States that we must now turn, as there cannot be a balanced perspective of postcolonial America without looking at how it has been perceived as a colonial or imperialist force today.

Growing respect for American dialects

One feature of a postcolonial society, especially in its initial stage, is the lack of respect accorded to its language or dialect used by the people. The low regard towards American English by Americans has been noted above. Over the decades (or perhaps, over the centuries), American English, especially with reference to some of its spoken varieties, has undergone what can best be described as the gradual increase of respect accorded to it. In this regard, Richard Bailey has suggested that American English is the paradigmatic example of how a variety of English can gain respectability. To him, 'Language communities thought to use debased varieties of English – for instance, the United States in the early nineteenth century – have later emerged as centers of vitality and elegance' (Bailey 1991: ix). Some varieties of American English today are as respectable as the more prestigious varieties of British English.

American cultural imperialism

When discussing the English language and cultural imperialism, it is not always the case that it is the English language itself which is at fault. In recent years, the English language is perceived as an agent of cultural imperialism largely through American political power. The United States might have been a latecomer to imperialism, but it is not traditional imperialism with a conventional army, as the United States did not physically conquer as large an area of the earth as Britain. It is imperialism that functions, in Loomba's words (1998: 111) 'through remote control'. This new type of imperialism is more dominant and powerful in the world today than the more conventional type of imperialism found in the past, but is less visible or obvious. One of the ways it manifests itself is, in Derek Walcott's words, by 'McDonaldizing everything' and 'Kentucky Frying everything' (1986: 204). It presents what Hall has described as 'essentially an American conception of the world' (1991a: 28). More negatively, it sidelines other world views, and renders them irrelevant, or even extinct. The South African novelist Nardine Gordimer describes American cultural imperialism in her country as 'terrifying' (Gordimer and Clingman 1992: 144).

Is American cultural imperialism linguistic?

Even though the English language, largely through American influence, is regarded as oppressive in the contemporary world, American cultural imperialism is not entirely linguistic. It is not exclusively centred on the English language *per se*, and although American accents and American varieties of English may play a part in it, these aspects of culture are often inextricably combined with other aspects of American cultural and political dominance. Indeed, highlighting the fact that it is not the use of the English language itself that is at fault, other English-speaking peoples, including the British, have also complained about American cultural imperialism. In 1999, four top Scottish authors of children's books tried to stem the spread of Americanisms into the language of young children in Scotland by making a video which they hoped would boost the children's Scottish accents. Their effort, which was supported by the Scottish Arts Council, arose out of the concern with 'the domination of American culture via television programmes like Sesame Street and Disney cartoon epics such as The Lion King' (Fraser 1999: 6). Thus, it is not merely American accents or other linguistic 'Americanisms' that they want to counter, but American cultural dominance as a whole.

The other mainly Anglo-Saxon cultures had to contend with the overwhelming influence of British culture earlier in their history, but it is interesting to see that the threat to national identity is now perceived as coming from America. America, unlike Britain, does not share the image of being the mother country or countries held by the other white settlers of Anglo-Saxon origin. So, from an emotional angle, the perception of an American threat to their cultures is more strongly felt. At any rate, the direct influence of British culture has receded during the course of the twentieth century. Furthermore, many aspects of culture originally from Britain, including the English language itself and many of the features associated with it, are now so assimilated into the cultures of the white settler colonies that they are not regarded as foreign elements, and are therefore not perceived as a threat.

The threat posed by American culture to the white settler colonies is perhaps most strongly felt in Canada, which shares a long common border with the United States. Gilbert and Tompkins (1996: 283) have noted that 'The political, economic, and cultural ties between the two countries have long positioned Canada as a nation which most constantly struggles to avoid being subsumed by its more powerful neigbour'. They mention the play, *The Farmers' Revolt* by Rick Salutin and Theatre Passe Muraille, in which an American invites a Canadian farmer to bring down the whole of Canada to the United States.

The problem with American cultural imperialism is that it is combined with other aspects of American power, and it is difficult to separate these from the purely cultural or linguistic aspects. For example, the debate on American influence in Australia also included the question, which was in the forefront in the 1920s, of whether American movies should be imported. As the movies in the 20s were silent, language, quite clearly, was not an important issue. The written language in the inter-titles, which are used to indicate what is said in the dialogue of silent movies, hardly differs from standard British English, and was certainly not a cultural problem.

The difficulty of separating other aspects of American cultural imperialism from the purely linguistic aspects can also be seen outside the white settler colonies. Gilbert and Tompkins (1996: 282) describe Walcott's play *Beef, No Chicken* as enacting 'not only a critique of American culture but also a subversion of its authority'. They also commented on another Caribbean play, Sam Selvon's *Highway in the Sun*, in which American troops built a road across a village in Trinidad, but are often not present on stage. It is clear that American power in the play, in spite of its stage absence, has a symbolic significance, as it 'undercuts the singular authority of the dominant culture' of Trinidad (Gilbert and Tompkins 1996: 279) and continues to exert its influence even without being physically present.

English literature or literature in English?

With the spread of English and literature written in the language outside Britain, another question that crops up is what kind of English ought to be used. Again, the American situation may have set the precedent for other literatures. A distinct variety of American English that was not comprehensible to non-American speakers of English was generally avoided in American literature. The language of *Huckleberry Finn*, which was not too difficult to understand by non-American speakers of English, was the exception rather than the rule, even when compared with Twain's use of language in his other fictional works.

Looking at the other settler colonies, a similar situation can be found. Grahame Johnstone (1967: 19), for example, has noted that in Australian literature, the 'peculiarities of pronunciation, vocabulary and syntax ... constitute a very small proportion of our speech, and even less of our written language'. Johnstone adds that 'even in its *colloquial* form, Australian English consists overwhelmingly of words and phrases which it shares with Standard English' (1967: 19); by 'Standard English' here, Johnstone obviously refers to what is now more commonly known as standard British English. Thus, bold linguistic experiments, such as that undertaken by Mark Twain in *Huckleberry Finn*, appear to be very much a minority interest not only in the United States but elsewhere in the white settler colonies. There is clearly a stronger urge in the white settler colonies to preserve English as it is used in Britain, when compared with the other former British colonies.

Problematic case of South Africa

An interesting case where the division between the white settlers and other colonised peoples is seen within a single country is South Africa. The literature of the white population belongs to that of the white settlers, whereas the literature of the black population is similar to literatures in English by the black people in other African states and by other writers in the 'Third World'. This is the 'solution' provided by Ashcroft *et al.* (1989), and by Skinner (1998) among others. However, Rosemary Jolly (1995: 21–3) is quite right in reminding us that this smacks of *apartheid*, which is the term used to refer to racial segregation which was practised before the 1990s in South Africa. In this regard, it must be noted that ever since the emergence of the mainly black African National Congress as the ruling party of South Africa in 1994, the country itself had abandoned *apartheid* as an official policy.

However, in spite of the criticisms of the division, trying to deny it altogether may not be totally defensible, even on political grounds. The non-division may also not be helpful in linguistic and literary analyses, as there are still fundamental differences between the white settlers and the blacks in terms of their attitudes towards language, the language they speak and write in, and the kind and content of the literature they produce. In the view of the black South African poet Mongane Wally Serote, 'every political system develops its own parlance, its own vocabulary, its own language' (McCord 1993: 184). The difference in language between the two groups can be seen in the conversation between a black South African farm worker and the white main character of J.M. Coetzee's *Disgrace* (1999: 201), which is a novel largely written in standard South African English:

> There is a long palaver of greetings that ought to be gone through, but he is in no mood for it. 'Lucy tells me the boy is back again,' he says. 'Pollux. The boy who attacked her.'
>
> Petrus scrapes his knife clean, lays it down. 'He is my relative,' he says, rolling the *r*. 'Now I must tell him to go away because of this thing that happened?'
>
> 'You told me you did not know him. You lied to me.'
>
> Petrus sets his pipe between his stained teeth and sucks vigorously. Then he removes the pipe and gives a wide smile. 'I lie,' he says. 'I lie to you.' He sucks again. 'For why must I lie to you?'

We can see the difference between the language used by the farm worker Petrus and the protagonist of the novel, who is a former university lecturer. Petrus rolls his 'r' for example. He does not resort to the interrogative mood in the question, 'Now I must tell him to go away because of this thing that happened?', instead of 'Now must I tell him …'. Petrus does not use the past tense in ' "I lie," he says. "I lie to you." ', when clearly the event is supposed to have occurred in the past. However, it can be argued that the lack of the interrogative mood here, considering that Petrus uses the mood at the end of the passage, may be a rhetorical device to prevent the protagonist from giving him an answer. It can also be argued that the avoidance of the past tense may be rhetorical as well, as Petrus uses it elsewhere ('this thing that happened'), and the present tense is probably intended to refer to Petrus's own version of the event: that he did not lie.

Of course the difference between the black farm worker and the white former university lecturer may be partly due to educational differences, but the conversation is emblematic of a wider racial division.

Educational difference itself is based on several decades of deliberate discrimination in educational language policy, in which black South Africans were treated as mere 'hewers of wood and drawers of water' and, it was argued in the South African Senate, that 'it is of no avail for him [the black South African] to receive a training which has as its aim absorption in the European community', such as training to ensure a good command of English (Reagan 1987: 302). The difference in attitude towards English may also be based on the fact that English is more precious in the eyes of the white community of British descent. English is not the main language of the majority of black South Africans, and to many of them it is only one of several languages existing in South Africa.

Influence of English or European models in early writings

Mazisi Kunene (1996: 14) has made the following strong observations about the dependence of the language of the South-African white settlers on European models or ways of seeing:

> ... non-African South African literature is characterised stylistically and thematically by an imitative quality derived from its European influence. This influence is even deeper than that which affected Australian, American, and Canadian literatures. ... South African literature, particularly in English, remains on the whole obsequious to the European models.

Nevertheless, in the words of Coetzee (1988: 8), there is a search, in the English-language South African literature of the white settlers, for a language 'to fit Africa'. However, Coetzee (1988: 8) notes that:

> English carries echoes of a very different natural world – a world of downs and fells, oaks and daffodils, robins and badgers – partly because English makes no claims (as Afrikaans does) to being native to Africa ...

Australian identity and language

English and the difficulties of creating an Australian identity

A similar desire to preserve the language against too many local influences is seen in Australian literature. In nineteenth-century Australian literature, there is no text comparable to Mark Twain's novel in either aesthetic quality or the creation of a nationalistic impact via the use of language. The nearest that one can find is Rolf Boldrewood's *Robbery Under Arms* ([1888] 1947):

> And his wife and the young 'uns 'll run out when they hear father's horse, and want to hear all the news. When he goes in there's his meal tidy and decent waiting for him, while he tells them about the poor chap he's been to see as is to be scragged next month. Ha! ha! what a rum joke it is, isn't it?
>
> (Boldrewood 1947: 30)

But even here, the language is not as significantly different from British English as Twain's use of language in *Huckleberry Finn*. A 'rum joke' and being 'scragged', for example, are also found in British English. Moreover, in some of his other works, Boldrewood is not able to escape from the British ideal in his use of language and his depiction of the Australian countryside, and he was not in favour of the kind of Australian linguistic nationalism in literature advocated by the literary journal *The Bulletin* (Brissenden 1972: 15).

The lack of a sense of separation from the language of British literature is even more pervasive in many other Australian authors. In Australian late romanticism in the nineteenth century, it has been claimed that the poets worked hard 'to accommodate Australian experience (landscape, nature, life) to standard English stereotypes', which left 'lyric poetry tired and listless' (Elliot 1974: 25). For instance, the connection with Britain is made in no uncertain terms in the poem 'Australasia' by William Charles Wentworth, which proclaims that Australia is 'a new Britannia in another world' (Murdoch and Mulgan 1950: 2). However, there are problems when one wants to utilise the language of British poetry to describe the Australian landscape. As the Australian poet John Tranter (1996: 86) notes, the problem

> was how to describe Nature as movingly as the Poet Laureate Mr. Wordsworth, when the nature was all wrong: vast deserts, noble savages who threw sharpened sticks at you and died of measles and smallpox while you watched, animals that seemed to have been made up as a joke, and a terrifying variety of poisonous snakes, deadly spiders, and bloodthirsty sharks, as well as an invisible jellyfish whose agonising sting can kill you in five minutes.

The problem with the language of Australian poetry is not significantly different from that of the language of prose. In Henry Kingsley's novel, *The Recollections of Geoffrey Hamlyn* (1859), a sprinkling of lexical items closely associated with the Australian landscape, such as *sheep*, *blackfellows* (Aborigines), *kangaroos*, *kangaroo rats*, *opossums* (actually the *possums*), *emus*, *drought* and *bush-fires*, can be found. But Kingsley bases the new landscape on an ideal version of what he knew in Britain, as 'features of Australia are thinned and idealized into the English reader's version of a Scottish glen' (Walsh 1973: 112). The major characters of his narrative are in fact Englishmen, who, like Kingsley himself, eventually return home to England, the 'Motherland of the colonies' (Barrett 1947: 5).

Even in the twentieth century, there are problems if one tries to look for attempts at severing English from its original motherland and creating a postcolonial Australian identity through language. As in the past, the linguistic effort to create this identity is usually rather feeble, and limited to vocabulary. As noted by a reviewer of two recent collections of Australian poetry, 'The Australianism of the poetry lies more in the depiction of landscapes with appropriate vocabulary than in particularly Australian language or revelation of an especially Australian cast of mind' (Gadd 1999: 831). For more sustained attempts at severing English from its colonial masters, one has to turn to minority writers, including writers of Aboriginal descent.

Aborigines and Australian literature

Language forms an important part of the literary art of Aboriginal authors writing in English, as they view it as an instrument of oppression. Although there were the only people on the continent before British colonisation, they have now become a minority of about only 1% of the population of the country. Their lower number today also has an effect on their languages: of the more than 250 Aboriginal languages that were believed to have been spoken at one time, only 100 remain, and seventy of the surviving languages are endangered. Some of the endangered languages are quickly dying, to the extent that the linguist Robert Dixon, for example, claims that some of them are dying quicker than he can record them (Preston 1990). The influence of Aboriginal languages on Australian English, as pointed out by the lexicographer W.S. Ransom, is also significantly less than that of Maori on New Zealand English (Preston 1990).

Although English is recognised by many Aborigines as the language of the colonisers, some of them write literary works in the language. Indeed, it may be the only language that they are able to write literary works in. Australian Aborigines harbour a suspicious attitude not only towards English, which some of them try to adapt in their written work in relation to the Aboriginal languages or dialects of English they speak, but also to the process of editing by white people. In order to write their works in a language or languages of their own, and to prevent themselves from being written about without consultation, a group of Aboriginal community leaders in the Kimberleys in Western Australia founded the publishing firm Magabala Books.

One example of a book published by Magabala Books is Glenyse Ward's *Wandering Girl* (1987). A white or non-Aboriginal editor might make some interventions on the language, which would affect its colloquial flavour, and which would in turn have a negative effect on the quality of the prose writing. For instance, in the following, the phrase 'to have a good old yarn to him' might be changed to 'to have a good chat with him' to make it conform to more 'standard' English:

> I was longing to have a good old yarn to him as he was the kind of person who made me feel differently from the rest of them around the farm. So I asked him if he would like a cup of tea?
>
> (Ward 1987: 63)

It can also be added that the question mark in the second sentence above might be deleted, as the sentence is not in the interrogative mood. However, much of the colloquial flavour of the language might be lost if these were done.

Likewise, an editor might change the apparent imperative mood in the third and final sentence of the following paragraph to the declarative: 'She would have to peel all the fruit ...'. Again, this would have affected the flavour of the original, which would also have an adverse effect on the quality of the prose:

> Another two hours and the boss would be back. I still had a couple of jobs to do. First, peel all the fruit and cut it up, then go out and water all the gardens, the front and back, then go and collect the eggs, then back into the house to get things ready for their tea.
>
> (Ward 1987: 67)

Aborigines in white writing

The importance of the Aborigines is also seen in literary works by white authors. A group of poets in the 1940s called the 'Jindyworobaks' tried to interpret the Australian environment directly , and not as a deflection of an ideal European or English landscape. Even though the Jindyworobak movement did not survive, it had an influence on subsequent Australian poetry. One of the finest Australian poets of the twentieth century, Judith Wright, has been described as feeling 'almost Aboriginal' in her depiction of the Australian landscape (Zinn 2000).

In the novel, a famous example of engagement with the Aborigine is Thomas Keneally's *The Chant of Jimmie Blacksmith*, which has also been made into a movie. While the engagement with the Aborigine in poetry is by presenting the landscape through native eyes, the engagement in the novel is through the introduction of more important Aboriginal characters. In both, however, the engagement with language may not be significant. At most, it may be through the use of non-standard English by the Aboriginal characters. However, the English used may not be unique to Aboriginal speakers of English, and may be more international in character. This is seen Jimmie's use of the 'n' instead of the 'ng' [ŋ] sound, and his use of the 'a' indefinite article instead of its 'an' variant before nouns or adjectives which begin with vowels: 'Unless I was workin' for a evil man. A man from Merriwa district, a unjust man' (Kenneally 1972: 48).

Clearly, language is only one of several factors that keep the Aborigine apart from the mainstream white population. In David Malouf's *Remembering Babylon* (1994), a white character, Gemmy Fairly, lives, from the age of thirteen, with Aborigines for sixteen years. Upon his return to the white community, he is not fully accepted, as he appears 'black' to them:

> For the fact was, when you looked at him sometimes he was not white. His skin might be but not his features. The whole cast of his face gave him the look of one of Them
>
> (Malouf 1994: 40)

Indeed, to the uninformed, language may play a more central role in differentiating the Aborigine than should be the case:

> He spoke five languages. His jaw, over the years, had adapted itself to the new sounds it had to make. Mightn't it happen after a time that the whole cast of a man's features would be shaped by that, the way a Frenchman, for instance, differs in his whole facial form from the Englishman or a Scot, and so come to share a likeness with the other speakers of the tongue?
>
> (Malouf 1994: 40)

Anglo-Saxon Australia and the linguistic experience of immigrants

It is interesting to note that although Malouf's paternal grandparents were Arabic-speaking immigrants, he himself has no problems associating himself with white Australia: 'I was born in Queensland, I grew up in Brisbane, my father was born in Australia, I see myself as absolutely Australian.' (Battersby 1996: 2). However, this is not the experience of many first-generation immigrant authors, for whom being an Australian is not so straightforward. Very often, the language problem is at the forefront of their desire to attain an Australian identity.

Among the examples of literary works dealing with the experience of first-generation immigrants is Dewi Anggraeni's novel *Journeys through Shadows* (1998). The English lessons taken by Maryati, the main character in the novel, play a prominent part in her struggles to understand, and to belong to, Australia. Maryati, like the author herself, is an immigrant from Indonesia. Although Maryati's struggles with English are a consequence of her being originally a non-English speaker, even English-speaking immigrants have problems with the attainment of an Australian identity, as there are differences in the dialects or accents of English they know and Australian English. The disjunction between dialects of English can be seen in the novel *Love and Vertigo* by Teo Hsu-Min (2000), who is from Malaysia and Singapore. There is the repeated realization in Teo's novel that one has to attain an Australian accent in speaking English in order to be accepted as Australian.

New Zealand

Division of literature

The division between literature in English written by the white settlers, and by the native population, is also seen in New Zealand literature. More specifically, it involves the division between literature in English by the Maoris, and by the Pakeha, which is a Maori word used to refer to white New Zealanders. Maori is an official language in New Zealand, and the county is officially bicultural. However, Maoris do not only write in their language, and writers in English of Maori descent, such as Patricia Grace, Witi Ihimaera and Keri Hulme, are widely known not only in New Zealand, but also across the English-speaking world. Some Pakeha writers are of course widely known, such as Katherine Mansfield, Fleur Adcock and Janet Frame. Mansfield, who is often regarded as one of the finest short story writers in the language, is in fact not often thought of as a New Zealand author. There is a difference in the cultural assumptions of each group, which affect the language used, in spite of the fact that New Zealand English is more strongly influenced by Maori when compared with the influence of the Aboriginal languages on Australian English.

The importance of the oral tradition in Maori literature

One difference between the literature in English written by the Pakeha and by the Maori is the firmer grounding in the works of Maori writers on oral literature and its more intense connection to the beliefs and myths of the Maori. In fact the Maori might have broken an age-old taboo by writing literature instead of reciting it (McRae 1991). Some Western beliefs and myths, including those imperceptibly embedded in nursery rhymes, are not pertinent to the Maori. For example, as a child, Witi Ihimaera did not understand why he had to learn nursery rhymes which were incompatible with his own cultural beliefs. He did not understand why 'Jack and Jill's well was located at the top of the hill, or why Little Miss Muffet was frightened by a spider'. According to Ihimaera, 'We Maoris put wells at the bottom of hills. We Maoris talk to spiders' (Helmi 1999: 11). As another example, the following address to a tree would rarely be found in poems by Pakeha or white poets in general. It is the first stanza of the poem 'No Ordinary Sun' by the major Maori poet in English Hone Tuwhare (1993: 28), from the book with the same title, originally published in 1964:

> Tree let your arms fall:
> raise them not sharply in supplication
> to the bright enhaloed cloud.
> Let your arms lack toughness and
> resilience for this is no mere axe
> to blunt nor fire to smother.

A comparable instance to the above in mainstream literature would be William Butler Yeats' paen to the chestnut tree in 'Amongst Schoolchildren':

> O chestnut-tree, great-rooted blossomer,
> Are you the leaf, the blossom or the bole?

But the address to the chestnut tree forms only a small part of Yeats's poem, and is there for a symbolic or illustrative purpose, quite unlike Tuwhare's poem, in which the address is sustained throughout the poem.

One senses that the use of the interrogative mood and the second-person pronoun in Yeats's poem is merely a linguistic/poetic deflection from the use of the third-person pronoun, whereas the use of the imperative ('... let your arms ...', 'raise them ...', 'Let your arms ...') and the second-person possessive determiner ('... *your* arms ...') in Tuwhare's poem is not merely a deflection: the entire poem deals with the persona's address to the tree.

Maori suspicion of the Pakeha

Historically, the Maori might have been treated less badly by the Pakeha when compared with the inhumane treatment of the Aborigine by the white population in Australia, and, as noted above, New Zealand English is more strongly influenced by Maori than Australian English is by the indigenous languages of that continent. However, a strong streak of suspicion can be found in the linguistic attitude of the Maori towards the Pakeha, and this is manifested in their literature written in English. Maori writers in English do not care too much if their works are not understood by the Pakeha and by other nationalities. According to Ihimaera, 'What's important is to tell your story with as much truth and honesty as you can and if you can have people outside of your community who can appreciate your works, then that is a bonus' (Helmi 1999: 11). Like the Australian Aborigine, Maori writers in English are also suspicious of Pakeha editing of their works and have set up their own publishing house. In 1991, the Huia publishing company was established, and it published its first novel in 1992. Huia was warmly supported by major Maori writers in English, such as Ihimaera and Patricia Grace (Moore 2000).

Canadian literature

Closeness to American cultural imperialism

Of all the major settler colonies, Canada is physically closest to the United States, and the effect of American cultural imperialism has been felt over a longer period of time, and with more immediacy, than in the other former settler colonies. One of the ways in which American cultural imperialism affects Canada is through the depiction of native American Indians in Hollywood movies. This has had an effect on the white Canadian attitude towards the native American, which is often manifested in the language used to describe them. One of the works that exploits and overturns the language used by Hollywood Westerns to describe the native American Indian is Jane Willis's *Geniesh: An Indian Girlhood*. According to Linda Warley (1998: 99), 'the language of Westerns provides Willis with a rich vocabulary'. In one episode, the author–narrator is ill with tonsillitis, and she says 'I awaited my death like a good little Indian' (1973: 93). Warley (1988: 99) has made the following apposite comment: 'The notion that the only good Indian is a dead Indian, is a notion that not only informed the plots of countless Westerns but also contributed to the actual murder of Native North Americans.'

The oral tradition in Canadian minority literatures

As in the other settler colonies, the oral tradition plays a prominent part in the works of native and other authors. The Okanagan storyteller Harry Robinson, for example, performed his stories before they were transcribed and translated for publication, although some features of the Okanagan language and of orality in general are retained (Marchand 1990). The oral tradition also has an effect on the literary genres chosen by native writers. The more prevalent genres of the works of native writers are poetry and drama. Poetry has structural similarities with some oral rituals (Lutz 1997), and orality is one of the inherent features of theatre, which has been described by Jean-Marc Dalpé as 'the privileged mode of expression of minority people' in Canada (Moss 1996: 77).

Loss of language

Like the Australian Aborigines, Canadian Indians also face the problem of language loss. As a result, one of the main themes of Canadian–Indian literature in English is the sense of regret at the death of their language, or the erosion of its functionality and the concomitant hatred of the white settlers for bringing about the decline or demise of their native languages, and for imposing their language on them (Lutz 1997).

One of the ways by which their native language is suppressed in schools is through the imposition of rules on native schoolchildren that punish them for speaking their own language. For example, in the primary school that Jane Willis (1973: 46) went to, the first rule was that 'There will be no Cree spoken in this school'. However, instead of following the rule, Willis and fellow Indian students remained silent and neither followed nor went against it. The author asserts their action, or, rather, non-action, parenthetically: '(This was a rule we absolutely refused to follow. By refusing to speak either Cree or English when any of the staff were around, we were able to escape punishment)' (Willis 1973: 46). As we will see in Chapter 7, the use of linguistic silence as a weapon against the colonialists is quite prevalent across the postcolonial world.

Linguistic suspicion of white Canadians

Like the Maori and the Australian Aborigines, Canadian Indian writers are linguistically suspicious of the white population. Some decades ago, many of their stories were heavily edited, in effect virtually retold by white editors. Like the Magabala Press in Australia and the Huia publishing company in New Zealand, Canadian Indians and other native peoples in Canada have also set up their own publishing company in order to publish their works. In 1980, Theytus Books was established in order to publish works by the Aboriginal people of Canada. It can be added here that the term 'Aboriginal' may be more appropriate than the term 'native', which has also been appropriated by the white settlers (correctly in some contexts): 'Aboriginal' refers to the original people of the land who were there before the arrival of white settlers, and in the context of Canada, covers both the Indian and Eskimo peoples. Like Magabala and Huia, the company was set up by Aboriginal Canadians and aims to publish more works by native Canadian authors and to avoid or lessen unnecessary or excessive editing by white editors.

Mixing languages

One consequence of the Canadian Indian suspicion of the white population is to use language in such a way that white readers may be linguistically left out. As noted above, a similar strategy is practised by the New Zealand author Ihimaera. Across the North American continent, native writers frequently resort to using two or more languages in their works, which are mainly in English (for a general discussion on mixing languages in literary works, see Chapter 8). Quite often, the non-English languages are not translated, or are not glossed elsewhere in the book.

Willis's *Geniesh* is a good example of this technique. The auto-biographical work is mainly in English, but also uses Willis's mother tongue, Cree. The passages in Cree are not directly translated into English and are not glossed in the book. Although the reader who does not understand Cree would be able to understand the general drift of the narrative, Warley (1998: 93) has noted that 'the white reader – like the white characters in the autobiography – is never completely privy to all of the exchanges between family members'.

In the following extract (Willis 1973: 40), which concerns the death of Willis's grandfather, the passages in Cree are indirectly translated. However, the exact nuance of the words used, or indeed whether the translation is merely a re-interpretation of the utterances in Cree, are a mystery to the reader who does not know the language:

'She [Willis' grandmother] wants me to interpret for her,' I said.
He [Reverend Dawson] sighed. 'Well, I suppose it doesn't make any difference now. What does she want?'
'jahgone natwhydimin isdook?' I asked my grandmother.
'jigjee-idt-danah eemhanooj-ah?' she asked.
'She wants to know if I can go to the funeral.'
'No! No! Absolutely not!' was his answer.
'nimwee ewe.'
'jahgaw-ewe ahk?' she asked, puzzled.
'She wants to know why not?'

Similarity with the Third World

The English writings of Aboriginal and other minority writers in the former settler colonies are not significantly different from those of 'Third-World' writers in general. Indeed, many of the features of postcolonial writing mentioned in this chapter will be mentioned again or developed further in later chapters, which deal more with writers from the Third World. The main difference between Third-World and Aboriginal writers may have more to do with demography than directly with language or literature: Aborigines have become a minority in the land that their ancestors have occupied for centuries or even millennia.

The relationship between Third-World and immigrant minority authors in English may be more obvious, as many of them were from former British colonies where English is a language used for the writing of literature. As a consequence, many of them are also considered writers of their countries of origin, such as – to look at the example of Canada – Sam Selvon and Neil Bissoondath from Trinidad, and Rohinton Mistry from India. Some of the writers have complex associations with the Third World, as the location of their ethnic origin is different from the location of their country of origin, such as Selvon and Bissoondath, who are ethnically South Asian Indians. Many of the writers have English as their first language, and some of them do not feel a sense of guilt in using English *per se*, but this is not universally the case. Canadian writers of Chinese ethnic origin, for example, may experience a sense of conflict in using English instead of Chinese (Clarke 2000: 131). Of course, writers who do not have a sense of conflict in using English itself may experience a clash between the types of English used. This conflict can be seen in the conflict between the use of Singaporean English and the establishment of an Australian identity in Teo's *Love and Vertigo* mentioned above, and the clash between Trinidadian English and other Englishes in the works of Selvon.

4 Orality, writing and what English brings

Moving beyond the white settler colonies, to the countries of the Third World, a different picture emerges. These countries are not as closely tied, emotionally or culturally, to England, and English is not the original native language of most people in the population, except perhaps for some countries in the Caribbean, where English, or rather a variety of the language, is used as a first language. For many of the non-Caribbean countries, it is more appropriate to talk of 'literatures in a borrowed tongue' when referring to their literatures in English. As such, they can be described as *non-native literatures*. The contexts for the analysis of these literatures, and the place orality, writing, and English as an imported language play in it, will be reviewed in this chapter.

The introduction of writing

As significant as the introduction of English in some of these countries, is the introduction of writing. Indeed, in some contexts it can be regarded as more significant. Ashcroft *et al.* (1989: 82), for instance, have asserted that 'In many post-colonial societies, it was not the English language which had the greatest impact, but writing itself'. In some of the societies that have languages without written scripts, the introduction of writing is as closely associated with colonialism as the introduction of English. For these languages, the romanised script, via English, was introduced for the purpose of writing. Of course, in territories controlled by other European powers, such as Spain and France, which also use the romanised script, similar situations apply.

However, the introduction of writing was not always a straightforward case of introducing a script to a language which did not have one, or giving people their first ever experience of reading and writing. Some of these languages used written scripts before the arrival of European colonialists. Ancient Akan, for example, which was spoken in West

Africa, had its own script, whereas Malay and Kiswahili used the Arabic script. The use of the ancient Akan script was lost over time, and the romanised script was introduced for Malay and Kiswahili because it was regarded as more linguistically appropriate than the Arabic script. The association of the introduction of writing with the colonial power may not be very strong in the cases of Malay and Kiswahili. A similar situation applied to Turkey, which was not colonised by a Western European power, but which also introduced the romanised script for the writing of Turkish, because of the belief that it was more efficient for writing the language. The substitution of the Arabic by the romanised script was opposed by some speakers of Malay, Turkish, and, as noted by Mazrui and Mazrui (1998b: 72–3), by speakers of Kiswahili as well, as the Arabic script had some traditional Islamic associations. Objections were raised not only on cultural grounds, but also, as in the case of Kiswahili, on linguistic grounds (Mazrui 1998: 45–6).

However, the romanised script, in most other instances, was introduced by the colonial power, or by bodies that had some association with it, to communities that did not have scripts for their languages. Among such bodies were the civil and educational services, and groups that took advantage of their governments' colonial control over other territories, such as missionaries.

The introduction and subsequent ascendancy of writing at the expense of speech can be distressing to some people. For example, in Buchi Emecheta's novel *The Joys of Motherhood*, the narrator observes that the two important characters in the narrative, Nnu Ego and Nnaife, 'were ill-prepared for a life like this, where only pen and not mouth could really talk' (1979: 179). In addition to the worry of not being able to cope with the written medium, there is also the fear – in some cases legitimate – that certain aspects of the oral tradition in general, or oral literature in particular, will simply disappear. The Zimbabwean author Tsitsi Dangarembga, for example, recalls the Zimbabwean independence celebration in 1980, when she heard 'the most beautiful poem I'd ever heard being recited'; it was in her native language, Shona, and it 'brought back to me that we have an oral language here' (Wilkinson 1992: 195). But she says that:

> ... it was also a painful experience for me: to think we'd lost so
> much of it. I sometimes feel that we need a programme, almost
> immediately, of sending out tape recorders and cassettes to any
> point possible and just asking people, old people in particular, to
> come in and just talk. It's all going. ... It was terribly, terribly sad.
> I found it very painful that this wealth of literature existed but it

hadn't been written down, and so one simply doesn't have access to it and it's being lost.

(Wilkinson 1992: 195)

What writing brings

Generally speaking, there was a transition from an oral to a literate culture in societies that did not have a written script before the arrival of the colonists. Arguably, with the introduction of writing, one may be able to glance at the beginning of literature itself as a written art form. In this regard, It has been claimed by Anthony West (1953: 22) that in reading Amos Tutuola's first novel, *The Palm Wine Drinkard*, 'One catches a glimpse of the very beginning of literature, that moment when writing at last seizes and pins down the myths and legends of analphabetic culture [i.e. a non-literate culture: a 'culture without an alphabet']'. This view is not comprehensively relevant to the Nigerian situation, as some of the indigenous languages in Nigeria, such as Hausa, Efik and Tutuola's mother tongue, Yorùbá, had written literary traditions of their own before the arrival of the European colonisers.

Whatever the extent of the relevance of West's observation, the introduction of writing brought with it new literary genres not possible in cultures that were largely based on the oral tradition. One example of a literary genre made possible by writing is long non-poetic narratives. In the oral tradition, long narratives are usually in poetic form. This is because poetic devices such as rhyme and regular metrical patterns act as mnemonic tools. In other words, these devices are helpful for remembering the lines of the narrative. Often, these long poems are also meant to be sung. Without the aid of a written text, certain salient features of the poetry and music found in the narrative poem help one to keep in mind the various details of the story.

Although writing may be viewed by some as a linguistic advance, not all communities consistently view it as such. For example, the earlier black South African writers did not view writing with a great deal of respect, as, in their view, 'written literature violated one of the most important literary tenets by privatizing literature' (Kunene 1996: 16). To them literature 'was understood to possess value by being disseminated in communally organised contexts'. To attain or re-attain the sense of community, 'many old people who were not versed in writing asked those who could write to read the story to them' (Kunene 1996: 16). Thus in the earlier history of black South African literature, the dissemination of written literature was partly carried out orally.

From oral to written language

The introduction of writing does not always result in the concomitant creation of a written literature. It may, for example, be introduced in a hurry, without due consideration being paid to sound linguistic principles, especially pertaining to which dialect of the language is adopted for its written version. In this regard, the following questions must at least be asked before the attempts to commit the spoken language to writing:

- Is there a standard version of the language being used?
- If a standard language is available, is it to be used for the written version of the language?
- If there are difficulties with ascertaining the standard language, is the written version at least based on a dialect of the language that is comprehensible and is respected by the majority of speakers of the language?

Without asking the above questions, the result for the written version of the language may be quite disastrous. Here, for example, are Achebe's views (in Gallagher's words 1997b) on how the written version of his language, Igbo, was introduced by missionaries:

> Formal, standardized, written Igbo – like many other African languages – came into being as a result of the Christian missionaries' desire to translate the Bible into indigenous tongues. Unfortunately, when the Christian Missionary Society tackled Igbo, they employed a curiously democratic process: they brought together six Igbo converts, each from a different location, each speaking a different dialect. Working their way through a particular biblical book or passage, each in turn would provide a translation.
>
> As one might expect, the resulting compilation bore no resemblance to any one of the six dialects. Yet this 'Union Igbo,' as it was called, authorized by repeated editions of the Bible, became the official written form of the language, a strange hodge-podge with no linguistic elegance, natural rhythm or oral authenticity.

Thus Achebe, like the eighteenth-century writer Olauda Equiano, who was also an Igbo, had to write in English, although for different reasons. As a slave who was later freed in England, Equiano had virtually no choice, as Igbo had not been written down at that time, and, even if it had been, there was no audience at all for the language in England.

Unlike Equiano, Achebe had a choice of languages, at least

superficially, and had written some poems in Igbo. But he faced a great deal of difficulty in writing his works in Igbo, because of the anomalies resulting from the method of introducing written Igbo. The effect of 'the long-standing controversy over an acceptable orthography', which 'remains unresolved to this day' had a comprehensive effect not only on Achebe, but also on the Igbos and their literature in general, as they 'have come to see and accept English ... as the language of Igbo literature' (Emenyonu 1978: xiv). Even the translation of literature into Igbo was difficult, so that Achebe's novels could not be easily translated from English into his native language as it now stands. Nevertheless, the rendering of Igbo proverbs in English, which forms an important part of most of Achebe's novels, is not always clear-cut. The author not only translates from one language to another, but 'from a spoken to a written culture', and as soon as the proverbs are written down, 'what has been a signpost becomes a monument' (Young 1973: 40).

The persistence of orality

Oral literature has persisted in written literature in many of the colonies not dominated by the white settlers. The Ugandan poet Okot p'Bitek, for example, was strongly influenced by indigenous oral traditions in his poetry. In relation to Samoan literature in English, Jacqueline Bardolph (1984: 51) has noted the following about its major writer Albert Wendt:

> In his best works one can hear echoes of the oral rhythm of traditional texts, and of the spoken voice generally. He is not just transcribing patterns of speech, but achieves an effective stylisation of oral characteristics for the written medium. ... He is the true heir of the Samoan storyteller, the tusitala, in that he can reproduce in dialogue many characteristic modes of speech ...

Among West African scholars, Chinweizu and Madubuike (1975, 1983) have asserted that critics of African literature should be more mindful of the importance of oral traditions in Africa, and of their contribution to the development of modern African literature. In this regard, writing is not separate from orality, but there is what Edouard Glissant has described as 'the complex union of writing and orality' (cited by Rodríguez 1996: 34), with the indigenous oral tradition making an important contribution to the conception of the written text. Glissant is referring to the Caribbean, where the African influence is significant, and where this union of the oral and written media can clearly be seen.

In this regard, it has been observed that 'a whole variety of fusions and amalgamations of these two media can be witnessed throughout the length and breadth of the Caribbean basin' (Rodríguez 1996: 36).

Turning back to Africa proper, the Ghanaian poet Kofi Anyidoho has made the strong claim that 'the fundamental impulse of my work derives from the oral poetic tradition' (Wilkinson 1992: 15). He specifies that 'the primary source of influence and interest for me has been the Ewe oral tradition' (Wilkinson 1992: 8). In Nigeria, Izevbaye (1974: 140) has noted that:

> The oral tradition is an important background to the literature because it is the first experience of literature for most Nigerians. Although the oral form of transmitting literature exists in all cultures it is more alive and more strongly felt in a country like Nigeria than in countries with longer histories of literacy. It is therefore more often treated by writers as the primary, though not necessarily more accessible, literary tradition

Arguably, Izevbaye's view should be qualified, as elements of orality persist even in cultures that have used written scripts for hundreds of years. This can be seen in former British colonies, where English exists side by side with other languages that have written scripts, but which still survive as largely spoken languages, as in Irish Gaelic and its relationship with English in Ireland today. In fact, this aspect of the relationship of Irish with English has been used by Bruce King to make a comparison between Anglo-Irish literature and African literature in English. In King's view, 'Irish writing in English is ... uniquely similar to African writing in its ability to incorporate a still living oral tradition within the forms of modern European literature' (1974: 16). After all, oral Irish Gaelic literature survived as a vibrant unwritten tradition until the middle of the nineteenth century, and it is not difficult to see both spoken Irish Gaelic and the language's oral literary tradition having a major influence on written Anglo-Irish literature. According to King, 'We are aware of the influence of Gaelic on the cadences of Anglo-Irish prose, the often un-British syntax and the way Irish writers seem rather to be talking than using print for rational, interpersonal discourse and narration' (1974: 16).

The introduction of writing does not necessarily mean the end of orality, or even of oral literature itself. Although some aspects of orality or oral literature have not survived, as in the case of the Shona oral tradition noted by Dangarembga above, other aspects continue to survive. However, these aspects may exist imitatively, within written literature rather than on their own, and live on as 'a sense of loss, an awareness of absence' (Gohrbandt 1996: 56). Nevertheless, this 'sense of loss' does not mean complete disappearance, but is a reminder of the continued viability of orality. Oral literature itself might have been lost in some postcolonial societies, but there are places where it continues to survive and thrive. In some societies, orality does not merely persist as an appendage or an imported quality found in written literature, but exists as living literature. Indeed, what appears as written literature abroad may also exist as oral literature in the countries of origin.

Another possibility whereby written literature does not signal the end of the oral tradition, but may in fact sustain it, is the reverse influence of written literature on oral literature, or the conversion of what was originally written into an oral form. Thus written literature does not kill off oral literature, but may give it a new lease of life. Indeed, a rigid distinction between the two may not work for many African societies, as they have a close symbiotic relationship (Barber and Moraes Farias 1989: 3). Ngũgĩ, for example, has made an interesting claim in an interview about his novel *Caitaani Mũtharaba-inĩ* (better known perhaps by the title of its English translation, *Devil on the Cross*) and his play *Matigari Ma Njirũũngi*, both originally written in Gĩkũyũ. According to Ngũgĩ, neither work remains as written literature but both have been appropriated into the oral tradition of the language (Jussawala and Dasenbrock 1992: 39). In a sense, Ngũgĩ is giving back to the oral tradition what he has taken from it, and the reverse influence is thus not one-way, as both works have been heavily influenced by the oral tradition.

In another interview (Wilkinson 1992: 129) Ngũgĩ relates how *Caitaani Mũtharaba-inĩ*, and to a lesser extent another work of his, the play *Ngaahika Ndeenda* (*I will Marry When I Want*) have become part of the Gĩkũyũ oral tradition:

> Now the reception of the novel and the play was really fantastic because they – particularly the novel – were read in buses, in *matatũs*, ordinary taxis; they were read in homes; workers grouped together during the lunch hour or whenever they had their own time to rest and would get one of their literate members to read for them. So in fact the novel was appropriated by the people and made part and parcel of their oral tradition.

It is interesting that the novel, which, unlike the play, more decidedly belongs to written literature, shows a stronger influence on Gĩkũyũ oral culture.

Oral literature continues to be vibrant in the Caribbean, even if it exists in a less traditional format. It has been observed that 'in most Caribbean countries, the concept of contemporary national poetry is associated with the notion of a literature that is to be heard, and with the image of a reciter who is able to attract a live audience (or, on many occasions, a crowd)' (Rodríguez 1996: 35). The recognition of the contribution of oral literature in the Caribbean has grown in recent years. This can be seen in the anthologies of Caribbean poetry produced between 1986 and 1989, where 'oral literature (anonymous or attributed) stands hierarchically alongside written literature' and where there is 'a common tendency towards the inclusion of performance poets' (Rodríguez 1996: 36). Instead of a process of denigration and diminution of oral literature, the supporters and practitioners of both written and oral literatures in the Caribbean are 'in the process of being granted recognition as equal-born personalities' (Rodríguez 1996: 37).

South Africa and Nigeria are two locations in Africa where oral literature continues to thrive. It has been noted that 'South African oral literature, like many African oral literatures, is one of the most vigorous and most elaborate extant in the world today' (Kunene 1996: 15). Modern technological advances do not seem to retard its progress, but seem to give it new possibilities of exposure:

> As [the credibility of South-African oral literature] is gradually restored by more common usage and exposure via television, radio, the stage, and the desacralisation of literality in modern life, oral literature and its traditions will earn a new respectability.
>   In recent years oral literature has flourished effectively in public stadiums and in more private venues.
>
> (Kunene 1996: 15)

The same reliance on technological advances to sustain the oral tradition is seen in Nigeria, where, in Gareth Griffiths words (1997: 140), 'the popular contemporary oral forms are turning to the modern high-tech inscriptive modes of television and film for their new lease of life'. Griffiths further notes (1997: 140) that 'It is in popular television series and programmes that you will find the most extensive use of traditional story or of fable, and the most widespread use of indigenous languages in contemporary representations of Nigerian society'.

Writing and politics

Is the introduction of writing innocent?

It can be argued that although the introduction of writing itself may be beneficial to the people of a previously non-literate scoiety, this is not the case if writing imposes itself upon the society in order to exert control over it. This is one of the arguments of Todorov's ([1974] 1987) *The Conquest of America*, which has been reiterated in the context of postcolonial literature by Ashcroft *et al.* (1989: 78–82). Another aspect of writing which can be viewed in a negative light is the sidelining of oral literary genres, which are viewed as *passé* by members of the community, as in the case of Shona oral literature in Zimbabwe, mentioned above.

However, the introduction of writing is not entirely negative. The fear that oral literary genres may be sidelined is not as great, as seen above, in Nigeria and in Zimbabwe's neighbour South Africa. It can also be noted that written literature itself may be used to depict spoken language. This is seen in the poetry of Edward Kamau Brathwaite and a number of other poets in the Caribbean. An important aspect of Brathwaite's conception of *nation language*, which will be discussed in greater detail later in the next chapter, is 'its emphasis upon, and validation of orality' (Walder 1998: 140). According to Brathwaite (1984: 17), *nation language*:

> ... is from ... an oral tradition. The poetry, the culture itself, exists not in a dictionary but in the tradition of the spoken word. It is based as much on sound as it is on song. That is to say, the noise that it makes is part of the meaning, and if you ignore the noise (or what you would think of as noise, shall I say) then you lose part of the meaning. When it is written, you lose the sound or the noise, and therefore you lose part of the meaning...

It is spoken rather than written language that clearly plays an important part in Brathwaite's poetry and that of a number of other Caribbean poets. This is a further illustration of the survival of orality in written literature, which was discussed earlier in this chapter. However it must be stated that the meaning presented in the written text is not as comprehensive as that presented in its oral form, or in song and performance, as meaning conveyed through facial gestures or hand movements cannot be included.

Although it can be said that oral literature has been sidelined by written literature, the latter may not be the only modern impediment to the endurance of oral literature. Radio, the cinema and television have also been blamed, although, as in the South African and Nigerian examples above, they may also be responsible for the survival of the oral tradition. However, English is a dominant language in cinema and on television. Thus the blame for the decline of the oral tradition in some literatures may be put on the widespread use of English on television or in the cinema, rather than on modern modes of communication *per se*.

Writing gives rise to nationalism

With the introduction of writing, an element not conducive to the continuation of colonialism is given shape. In this regard, Benedict Anderson has noted that 'Print-capitalism' as he calls it, is a vehicle for linking disparate communities or groups of people together and creating 'particular solidarities' (1991: 133) based upon a shared printed language. The written word 'made it possible for rapidly growing numbers of people to think about themselves, and relate themselves to others, in profoundly new ways' (1991: 36). These new ways include building a national consciousness. Images of homogeneity are then maintained by 'creating a community out of signs, not sounds' (1991: 13). The irony here is that the written language brought by the colonists became a force for a nationalism that could not have arisen without the introduction of writing.

What English brings

Bringing in or supplanting?

As seen above, the introduction of English and the introduction of writing may have an inextricable connection. For a non-literate culture, the introduction of English may indeed mean the introduction of writing at the same time. However, the introduction of English may be viewed in a more negative light when compared with the introduction of writing by itself. This is especially the case when it is effectively used to supplant the indigenous languages instead of introducing or adapting a written script for them.

Among languages that have been supplanted by English are the Aboriginal languages in Australia, many of which have become extinct. Many Australian languages did not merely die a natural death – which was the case with some languages in the colonies – but there was also a systematic attempt to eradicate them. Many Aboriginal children were taken away from their parents when they were young and were educated in English. They were then prevented from speaking their own language and were threatened with punishment if they did so. As a consequence, the language was not passed on to their children. This is not a simple loss of language, but, according to Gilbert and Tompkins (1996: 164), it 'leads to the possibility of a loss of names, of oral history, and of a connection to the land'. In effect, 'To name people and places in English, replacing any earlier constructions of location and identity, is to establish at least partial control [by the colonists] over reality, geography, history, and subjectivity' (Gilbert and Tompkins 1996: 165). The control or domination over local cultures – which goes hand in hand with the eradication of some of them – continues, at least symbolically, even after the granting of independence.

Gilbert and Tompkins (1996: 275) have noted a similar linguistic situation in New Guinea, where education has resulted in the death of native languages. The New Guinean play *Cry of the Cassowary*, by John Wills Kaniku, criticises the boarding school system in the country, whereby students at high-school level are sent away to places far away from their residence, some of which are in Australia. What results is a 'neo-colonial élitism', which 'is based on a hierarchy of values which stipulates that village culture is outdated and that western education represents the only worthwhile repository of knowledge'. As a result, whenever the children return to their villages, they tell their parents 'how good and educated they are' and 'how primitive we are' (Gilbert and Tompkins 1996: 275).

The system of punishment against the use of the native language, mentioned by Gilbert and Tompkins above, is certainly widespread. In Kenya, Ngũgĩ (1986: 11) recalls an undesired way by which English was imposed at the expense of native languages:

> ... one of the most humiliating experiences was to be caught speaking Gĩkũyũ in the vicinity of the school. The culprit was given corporal punishment – three to five strokes of the cane on bare buttocks – or was made to carry a metal plate around the neck with inscriptions such as I AM STUPID or I AM A DONKEY...

Ngũgĩ's native language, however, did not face the fate of the Australian Aboriginal languages. Not only did the language survive, but thanks partly to Ngũgĩ – who, as mentioned earlier, abandoned

English as the first language for creative writing and became a major writer in Gĩkũyũ – it survives as a language of written literature.

Bringing in new genres

Quite apart from the introduction of written literature itself, the introduction of English brought in new literary genres to some communities, or, brought in new themes or styles to their works. For example, the first novel written by an Indian, Bankimchandra Chatterjee's *Rajmohan's Wife*, which was published in 1864, was written in English. However, this influence was felt not only in relation to literary works written in English but in relation to those in indigenous languages as well. For example, O. Chandu Menon's *Indulekha* (1889) was one of the first novels in Malayalam. Menon wrote the novel for two reasons. First, it is an 'attempt to fulfil his wife's "oft-expressed desire to read in her own language a novel written after the English fashion". Second, Menon wants 'to see if he could create a taste for that kind of writing "among my Malayalam readers not conversant in English" ' (Loomba 1998: 75).

The influence of Western genres is felt not only in the early growth of the postcolonial literatures, but perhaps even more so in their later development. The models adopted in their later development are usually from more recent British literature, but, occasionally, they may also be retrieved from the earlier history of English literature. The contemporary poet David Dabydeen, for example, is influenced by medieval alliterative poetry originating from the north of England.

Usually, Western generic influences are mixed with more local influences, both generic and non-generic. Even Dabydeen is not influenced by medieval alliterative poetry from the north of England for its own sake. He adopts the medieval model because he finds the 'north/south divide of England an echo of the divide between "the so-called Caribbean periphery and the metropolitan centre of London" ' (Dabydeen 1990: 4). It can also be mentioned here that Brathwaite's conception of *nation language* specifically mentions that it 'largely ignores the pentameter' (1984: 13). So Caribbean poets, in their search for models in the writing of poetry in English, have to look elsewhere. According to Brathwaite, some Caribbean writers find it in the *calypso*, a popular song genre which originated in the region.

A mixing with local genres can also be seen in the work of the Nigerian novelist Amos Tutuola. Tutuola's work has been influenced not only by the Bible and Bunyan's *Pilgrim's Progress* but by oral Nigerian literature as well. There is thus an interplay between the influence of genres learned via the English language and more indigenous forms. Sometimes, the giving way of the influence of Western to more traditional genres can be seen from a developmental perspective. For example, the Nigerian poets John Pepper Clark and Christopher Okigbo 'both began by using English poets as models until they found their feet and later attempted to develop certain verse techniques found in vernacular poetry' (Izevbaye 1974: 151). However, it is not always easy to determine where one influence ends and another begins.

New genres arise not only in works written in the English language, but are introduced or developed under the influence of Western literary forms and in indigenous languages as well. The example of Menon's novel has been mentioned above. In the case of drama, local and foreign influences are closely connected. Bruce King (1992: 4) has questioned, for example, whether Maori theatre can 'evolve without European forms', and whether African theatre could 'be built directly upon African rituals and masquerades'.

What English brings and what is already there

As seen in the examples of the authors above, there is usually a mixture of influences – between the local and the imported English or Western strands, and it is sometimes difficult to draw the line between the indigenous and the imported, or to determine which is stronger or has the greater impact. The difficulty of drawing the line between the two strands is seen in Ben Okri's description (in Wilkinson 1992: 78) of some of his early readings, and how they are intermingled with local myths and stories told by his mother:

> My earliest readings were of folktales and myths, Greek myths, German myths, Roman myths, African myths, African legends. And my mother always told me stories. All of them were intermingled. I didn't separate one thing from the other. Aladdin was as African to me as Ananse. Odysseus was just another variation of the tortoise myth.

Another example is of the difficulty of isolating the local and the foreign influences on the Bible and Christianity, where, surprising as it may seem, the local and the foreign are sometimes hard to distinguish. The Bible and Christianity as a whole are an important concern, as they are among the most significant influences on many works of African literature in English. Christianity was, in many instances, introduced to the African colonies via imperial conquest, and, more specifically in the British colonies, via the English language. However, its pervasion of some indigenous African societies has ensured that it cannot be entirely certain whether any symbolism, words or proverbs borrowed from the Bible are due to non-indigenous influences. Quite often, these elements from the Bible are so deeply entrenched in the society, and inextricably intertwined with indigenous influences, that the division between the local and the foreign cannot confidently be made. Because of the infusion of the Biblical elements in the society, the writer has to refer to them, even if he is not a believer. As Ngũgĩ has noted (in Wilkinson 1992: 130):

> ... I use the Bible quite a lot, or biblical sayings, not because I share in any belief in the Bible, or in the sanctity of the Bible. It's just simply as a common body of knowledge I can share with my audience, and the same is true when I'm writing in Gĩkũyũ language, I use the Bible quite a lot.

Another area where it is difficult to sort local and foreign influences into separate categories is the tragic sense in some postcolonial literary works. For instance, the tragic sense in Nigerian fiction should not only be seen in terms of an indigenous Nigerian world view, but it can also be traced back to ancient Greek tragedy. Classical Greek drama has a stronger influence in Nigeria than elsewhere, and it can be seen in the work of Wole Soyinka and Ola Rotimi. Gilbert and Tompkins (1996: 38) have attributed the strong influence of classical Greek drama there to Nigerian theatrical practice, which, like that of ancient Greece, maintains 'strong roots in ritual and festival'. A similar confluence of ancient Greek and local cultures can be seen in the blend of Greek myths and legends centred on the Aegean Sea and those of the Caribbean in *Omeros* and *The Odyssey* by the St Lucian poet and playwright Derek Walcott.

It has also been argued, giving more significance to the impact of inherited or indigenous influences, that:

> the text that reverberates most influentially at the heart of [V.S. Naipaul's] *A House for Mr. Biswas* is not from the Western tradition. It is, instead, the Ramayana, one of the two sacred Hindu texts, the Mahabharata being the other. According to R.K. Narayan, all imaginative writing in India has its origins in these books.
>
> (Wong 1996: 199)

With reference to Naipaul's earliest works, it has been said that his 'original comic vision ... owes much to his story-telling Hindu forebears and the creole street talk of his native Port-of-Spain' ('A Song of Lost Islands'). The same can be said about the importance of indigenous influence in the presence of the Vedantic tradition in Raja Rao's *Serpent and the Rope*. Indeed, in a fundamental sense, Derek Walcott has observed that 'What is inherited by Salman Rushdie, V S Naipaul, Michael Ondaatje, Ben Okri, and so on, is a sharing that has nothing ultimately to do with England' (Benjamin 1995: 30). The idea of 'sharing' here is viewed negatively. In this regard, Walcott further explains that 'When I meet Salman Rushdie, Wole Soyinka, or Michael Ondaatje, we are sharing a language, but more than that, we're sharing an experience that has evolved out of the idea of the Empire and that hasn't pained us' (Benjamin 1995: 31). This may be a negative way of looking at the whole question of 'influence': what England *did not* really give, or what she was at best only able to 'give' indirectly.

In trying to untangle the difference between what English brings and what is already there, it is not only the balance between the local influences and the English or European influences that must be struck. Certain English or European ways of perceiving reality, which may not match the reality of the local situation, must also be got rid of. This was a major problem with writers from the settler colonies, where their perception of the local scene was filtered through some stereotypes or tropes learned from English literature. However, these stereotypes or tropes did not match the local situation and landscape and had a negative effect on the quality of the literature.

This problem, although greater in the settler colonies, is by no means confined to them. The English language itself, with its long and deep-rooted literary tradition, may not be readily helpful. As the Caribbean poet Kamau Brathwaite (1993: 263) has noted, 'we haven't got the syllables, the syllabic intelligence, to describe the hurricane, which is our experience; whereas we can describe the imported alien experience of the snowfall'. However, the hurricane 'does not roar in pentameter' (Brathwaite 1993: 265). Similarly, the writer Michelle Cliff (1985: 13), who is of Jamaican origin, notes that in the poetry of some Caribbean poets, 'You have to dissect stanza after extraordinarily Anglican stanza for Afro-Caribbean truth; you may never find the latter'.

This problem is not confined to literary expression, but extends to the author's perception of reality, filtered, undoubtedly, by the earlier pedagogical exposure to what was then available in the English language and its literature. The novelist Sam Selvon (1987: 35), when he was in Trinidad, 'while reciting English verse under a mango tree in the schoolyard', dreamt in 'the hot tropical atmosphere' 'of green fields and rolling downs, of purling streams and daffodils and tulips, thatched cottages and quiet pubs nestling in the valleys'. His experience of the English countryside upon reaching England, was perhaps quite similar to that of the British sociologist Stuart Hall (1991a: 24), who was also from the Caribbean, and who emigrated to England when he was a child:

> When I first got to England in 1951, I looked out and there were Wordsworth's daffodils. Of course, what else would you expect to find? That's what I knew about. That is what trees and flowers meant. I didn't know the names of the flowers I'd just left behind in Jamaica.

Daffodils, and their association with Wordsworth's poetry, have frequently been used as a convenient emblem for what cannot (or should not) be found in poetry in English written outside England, especially in the tropics, where they cannot be found. As noted earlier, Coetzee finds that daffodils, which are closely associated with the English language as contrasted to Afrikaans, are alien to the South African experience. In literature education, daffodils were inadvertently used to represent what children were actually not able to be sympathetic to, as they could not find the flowers in their own country. In the words of Gilbert and Tompkins (1996: 15), 'William Wordsworth's poem, "I Wandered Lonely as a Cloud," was taught to uncomprehending West Indians, Kenyans, and Indians who had never seen a daffodil'. According to Naipaul a daffodil, before he went to England, was a 'pretty little flower no doubt', but as one had not seen it in Trinidad, he asks rhetorically, could Wordworth's poem 'have any meaning for us?' (1972: 23).

Many West Indian authors are not free from the problem of finding their vision of their birthplace's landscape obscured or distorted by what they have read in books by British authors. This problem was faced, and later overcame, by Walcott, who, like Selvon, Hall and Naipaul, also came from the West Indies:

> His own excellent education gave him access to the riches of English literature, which has been a powerful influence on his poetry. Yet there was always something odd about it. It was strange to have to learn Wordsworth's famous poem by heart without having seen a daffodil in one's life. None of the trees so common in English poetry existed on the island. The young Walcott had to discover the

sensuous richness of St Lucia for himself and thus, like Adam, bring
a new world to life in his mind.

('A Song of Lost Islands')

It was only after Walcott brought 'a new world to life in his mind'
that his poetry achieved a higher quality. Similarly, the Zimbabwean
poet Musaemura Bonas Zimunya was influenced by the poetry of
Wordsworth in his early poetry, but was annoyed later in life by one of
his poems which ended 'with a little Wordsworthian hut'. According to
him, it was only after he read 'Ngũgĩ and Achebe and Senghor [that] it
suddenly occurred to me ... that there was something wrong in this
land that I was praising!' (Wilkinson 1992: 208).

Subverting the English and Western influences

Authors are quite often perfectly aware of what they borrow from the
West, as the case of Walcott illustrates. Indeed, quite often, what they
do is not to borrow English or Western models blindly, but to subvert
some of the assumptions underlying the themes, ideas or plot-lines. It
has been noted in this regard that 'a prominent endeavour among
colonial writers/artists had been to rework the European "classics" in
order to invest them with more local relevance and to divest them of
their assumed authority/authenticity' (Gilbert and Tompkins 1996: 16).
This tendency has been described by Helen Tiffin (1989) in terms of a
canonical 'counter-discourse', where canonical texts from the West are
interrogated or subverted. But what results from the counter-discourse
is quite often not a simple subversion or overturning of accepted
assumptions generated by the work. As Ashcroft *et al.* (1989: 33) have
noted, these works do not simply reverse 'the hierarchical order' that
the original works assume, but more fundamentally, they interrogate
'the philosophical assumptions on which that order was made'.

Among the texts that have been repeatedly subverted in this way is
Shakespeare's *The Tempest*. In Derek Walcott's *Dream of Monkey Mountain*,
for example, which makes use of the play, Shakespeare himself is tried
and hanged for crimes against humanity. Aimé Césaire's *Une tempête*,
although largely written in French, makes use of creole, Kiswahili and
English, thus subverting the main language of the play, English. The
basic plot of the above is compressed by Boehmer (1995: 205), who
gives further examples of the subversion of Shakespeare's work:
'Lamming's *The Pleasures of Exile* and *Water with Berries* (1971), Kamau
Brathwaite's *Islands*, and David Dabydeen's "Miranda/Britannia" poems

in *Coolie Odyssey* (1988), invert the perspectives of *The Tempest*, mainly by identifying with the bitter cursing of Caliban'. The subversion of Shakespeare's work often has a linguistic basis: Caliban's curses are in the language he learns from Prospero. In the words of Lamming (1992: 118–9) 'We shall never explode Prospero's old myth until we christen language afresh'. The subversion of *The Tempest* has not been exhausted, as seen in the more recent work *Reef*, by the Sri Lankan author, Romesh Goonesekera (for a more extensive discussion of postcolonial subversions of Shakespeare, see Cartelli 1999).

Another work from English literature that has been quite frequently subverted is Daniel Defoe's *Robinson Crusoe*, which has been described by Biodun Jefiyo (1989: 114) as 'a classic "megatext" of Eurocentricism'. From the perspective of English language pedagogy, Alastair Pennycook believes that 'it is perhaps always worth asking ourselves as English teachers to what extent we are following in Crusoe's footsteps' (1998: 11). The 'subversion' of Defoe's novel can be seen in J.M. Coetzee's *Foe* and the *Narrative of Jacobus Coetzee* in his collection *Dusklands* (Gardiner 1987), and also in Derek Walcott's collection of poems *The Castaway* (1965) and his play *Pantomime* (1980). In Coetzee's *Foe*, for example, the character who resembles Man Friday, instead of learning to communicate with Crusoe in pidgin English – which after all, is still a variety of English – is incapable of speech. He is thus not able to learn to communicate with Crusoe through spoken language, let alone in a simplified form of English. In Walcott's *Pantomime* (1980: 126), two characters discuss putting on a pantomime in which a black Crusoe 'comes across this naked white cannibal called Thursday, you know':

> This cannibal, who is a Christian, would start unlearning his Christianity. He would have to be taught ... I mean ... he'd have to be taught by this – African ... that everything was wrong, that what he was doing ... I mean for nearly two thousand years ... was wrong. That his civilization, his culture, his whatever, was ... *horrible*.
>
> [ellipses and emphasis in the original]

It must be added here that as Man Thursday's 'civilization, his culture, his whatever, was ... *horrible*', so is his language.

It is easy to see why both *Robinson Crusoe* and *The Tempest* have been frequently subverted, as each of them deals with a foreign individual informally occupying an island. He then displays a master–servant relationship with a native of the island and imposes his language on him. One response to learning the master's language is for the native to acquire it 'imperfectly', as in the case of Man Friday, who perhaps has the disadvantage of learning it as an adult; or maybe, as in the case of Coetzee's Man Friday character, learning it is a disadvantage and he whould be better off not learning it at all. Another response is for the native to learn it so well, as in the case of Caliban, that he speaks it more beautifully than his master, which does appear to be an allegory of the expansion of literatures in English outside England. The narrative of occupation and suppression of the native, including the imposition of the master's language, thus appears to be a reflection of the larger pattern of formal colonisation and imposition of the colonial language on the native population.

5   Using English in postcolonial literatures

A review of criticism

The question of why literature should be written in English is a perennial one in countries whose people do not speak English as a native language. One response is to ask whether English is a local language. This is the question asked in almost all countries where literatures in English are written. A related question to be discussed later in the chapter is whether works written in a borrowed tongue can result in literature that can be regarded as one's own.

Why should literature be written in English?

English as an African language

One of the questions asked in African literature in English was whether English was an African language (Desai 1993). In the 1960s, the South African writer Guy Butler insisted that English was an African language, which to Dorothy Driver was 'radical for the 1960s' (1996: 99). This claim may hinge on how long English had been used in the continent. However, even Achebe, a defender of the use of English in African literatures, has cast some doubts on the validity of this claim, as the use of English for writing literature may not depend on whether it is an African language, but may have a more practical basis:

> As you know there has been an impassioned controversy about an African literature in non-African languages. But what is a non-African language? English and French certainly. But what about Arabic? What about Swahili even? Is it then a question of how long the language has been present on African soil? If so, how many years should constitute effective occupation? For me again it is a pragmatic matter. A language spoken by Africans on African soil, a language in which Africans write, justifies itself.
>
> (Achebe 1975: 67)

Nevertheless, the use of English for literature may transcend merely practical considerations. According to Achebe 'The British did not push language into my face while I was growing up', as there is a political reason for learning the language and using it to write literary works. He chose to learn English and eventually to write in the language as a means of 'infiltrating the ranks of the enemy and destroying him from within' (quoted in Gallagher 1997b). Also, English 'enabled him to address a Nigerian audience, ... for he needed to use a lingua franca, not a tribal language such as Igbo.' There are approximately 150 indigenous languages in Nigeria, and English acts as the common language for many Nigerians: it enables them to read his work. The situation is different in East and North Africa, where there are local lingua francas shared by substantial percentages of the local population. We will return to the situation in East Africa shortly.

Achebe had another important reason for writing in English. Even if he had wanted to write in his native language, Igbo – in spite of its limited audience – he could not have done so. Granted, there are qualities in Igbo not found in English. As has been pointed out more than once by Nigerian literary critics, the translation of the Igbo word *dibia* as 'medicine-man' 'over-simplifies the functions and status of the *dibia* in Igbo traditional society' (Okonkwo 1979: 94; see also Young 1973: 25–6). Another problem, less perceptible on the surface but equally important, is the dilution of the flavour of the language when Igbo words and phrases are rendered in English. As noted by Buchi Emecheta, another eminent novelist of Nigerian origin whose mother tongue is Igbo, 'English sounds colourless and grey in translation' whereas 'Igbo uses colourful phrases, and the language itself will always remain closest to my heart' (Holmes 1996).

Achebe does have a similar emotional reaction to Igbo, and one suspects that – in spite of his staunch defence of the use of English in African literature – there is more than a tinge of embarrassment about his use of English instead of Igbo. In his novel *No Longer At Ease* (1960: 49), the main character, Obi Okonkwo, reflects on his use of English in England:

> It was humiliating to have to speak to one's countryman in a foreign language, especially in the presence of the proud owners of that language. They would naturally assume that one had no language of one's own.

As Achebe asks elsewhere (1965: 30), 'Is it right that a man should abandon his mother tongue for someone else's?' and replies, 'It looks like a dreadful betrayal and produces a guilty feeling'.

But in spite of Achebe's positive emotional attachment to Igbo, it is not possible for him to write effectively in the language. As mentioned above, when someone asked him if his *Things Fall Apart* had ever been translated into Igbo, he had to explain that the spoken language exists in numerous dialects, differing from village to village, and the written language is in fact a haphazard combination of these dialects. As a consequence, it is difficult for the written version of Igbo to be used for creative writing, and was in fact a hindrance to the development of written literature in the language (see Emenyonu 1978). Achebe had to confess that 'there is no choice' for him (1975: 62). Thus, not only was *Things Fall Apart* not translated into Igbo, but it could not have been originally written successfully in the language, even if Achebe had wanted to, and this also applied to the writing of his other novels.

English is not an African language

However, Achebe's views on the use of English in African literature have not gone unopposed. According to Obiajunwa Wali (1963: 14), 'the whole uncritical acceptance of English and French as the inevitable medium for educated African writing is misdirected, and has no chance of advancing African literature and culture'. Wali warns that 'until these writers and their western midwives accept the fact that any true African literature must be written in African languages, they would be merely pursuing a dead end, which can only lead to sterility, uncreativity, and frustration'.

A more prominent opponent is Ngũgĩ, who is not happy with the fact that 'languages of Europe (here, English) were taught as if they were our own languages, as if Africa had no tongues except those brought there by imperialism, bearing the label "MADE IN EUROPE" (cited by Yancy 1996). Ngũgĩ (1998: 78) in fact questions the use of English in another West African novel, the Ghanaian Ayi Kwei Armah's *The Beautyful Ones Are Not Yet Born*: 'It is interesting that a text which is so scornful of the adopted Oxbridge accent of the Ghanaian middle class should be conspicuously silent on the question of English as the language used, irrespective of the accent of the speakers.' To Ngũgĩ, the very act of using English is ultimately class-based, as the audience is restricted to 'the educated African elite or the foreigners who speak the language' and preclude 'the peasantry of Africa, or the workers in Africa who do not read or understand' the language (Martini *et al.* 1981: 113). In fact, by using English, the majority of the author's readership may very well be white, as emphatically encapsulated in the title of Phanuel Akubueze Egejuru's book, *Black Writers, White Audience* (1978); Egejuru's study deals with the predicament of African writers in English and French whose main audience is white.

So what can be described as the 'abduction' of English as an African language is not a smooth process, with some, like Ngũgĩ, viewing the belief that it could be 'abducted' as offensive. He is of the view that while 'The bullet was the means of the physical subjugation', 'Language was the means of spiritual subjugation' (1986: 9). According to Ngũgĩ, 'What is really happening now is that African thought is imprisoned in foreign languages' (Jussawalla and Dasenbrock 1992: 30).

Some of the finest novels in English to have come out of Africa have been written by Ngũgĩ, and he has been described by Jussawalla and Dasenbrock (1992: 9) as 'one of the great novelists in English of our time'. Nevertheless, as is well known, he later abandoned English for Gĩkũyũ for the purpose of writing original works. After writing his works in Gĩkũyũ, he translated them into English, although since 1987 he has stopped translating his own works. Ngũgĩ's attitude towards English is the opposite of Achebe's. According to Achebe, 'There's no point in fighting a language', but to Ngũgĩ there clearly is.

Ngũgĩ's position on the English language – and, by extension, on the British and on European civilisation as a whole – is not exactly an isolated one in the continent of Africa. The South African poet and scholar Mazisi Kunene has expressed similar opinions. Kunene (1968) views African writers' avoidance of their native languages in terms of what he calls *deculturation*. In the previous chapter, Kunene's defence of the indigenous oral literature in South Africa and his views on the dependence of the English language on Western modes of viewing reality were mentioned. In fact, even more comprehensively than Ngũgĩ, Kunene does not and did not write any of his original creative works in English. He wrote them in Zulu, and all the English versions of his poetry are actually translations from the original in Zulu, even though they read 'as beautiful poetry in English' (Wilkinson 1992: 137). However, Kunene's position is not representative of Southern Africa as a whole. The Zimbabwean writer Zimunya, for example, remarks that 'it's difficult for people in Zimbabwe to bother about what Ngũgĩ says about language, because we never had the problems Kenyans have'. As such, the language issue 'doesn't arouse any excitement or debate in Zimbabwe at all'. Zimunya reflects on his own situation: 'I am actually writing in my own language now, but you don't even think about it, you just write!' (Wilkinson 1992: 210).

Turning to the contrasting viewpoints of Ngũgĩ and Achebe, their positions on English can be taken as emblematic of a wider divide between East and West Africa. Nevertheless, the division is not clear-cut, as the issue of whether English should be used for creative writing has also been hotly debated in Nigeria itself. According to the Nigerian critic Femi Ojo-Ade (1989: 248), for example, European languages for the writing of African literature are 'the perfect vehicle of the cultural half-breed' (see also the discussion in Gohrbrandt 1996). The view of Obi Wale has been mentioned above. There was in fact an intense and sometimes acrimonious debate in post-independent Nigeria, with Wale's views as a focal point, on the use of English for the writing of literature:

> Throughout 1963 and 1964 there raged a battle about this issue mainly in the Accra-based magazine *Transition*. The chief instigator of the polemics was Obi Wale, who argued that for African literature to succeed it had to be rendered in an African language. To write in English would be to yield to the colonialist way of thinking; your values would be immersed with those of the white man, he claimed. This would eventually be the 'dead end of African literature' (to borrow the title of his article).
>
> (Granqvist 1984: 178; see also Benson 1986: 133–9)

Looking back, Achebe's defence of English was not a decontextualised stance, but he was practically 'provoked to defend his use of English.' Looking further back, it should also be said that Ngũgĩ's attitude towards the continued use of English should not be seen outside its context, as East Africa, unlike West and South Africa, did not have 'long periods of writing in English behind them' (Walder 1998: 54). Hence the need to defend its use was less established, as it had a shorter history.

English as an Indian language

The questions of whether English is one's language, and, if it is not, whether one should write literary works in it, are asked not only in Africa, but also in another important geographical location where writing in English thrived and continues to thrive with even greater strength towards the end of the twentieth century – India.

English has occasionally been regarded as an Indian language. According to Raja Rao (1963: vii), in the famous foreword to his first novel *Kanthapura* (1938), 'English is not really an alien language to us'. Rao (1963: vii) explains that 'It is the language of our intellectual make up – like Sanskrit or Persian was before'. R.K. Narayan, another significant Indian writer of fiction in English from an earlier generation (1988: 197), notes that Indian English is 'a legitimate development and needs no apology', and that the language 'is now undergoing a process of Indianization in the same manner as it adopted U.S. citizenship over a century ago' (1965: 123). Pritish Nandy, in his *Indian Poetry in English Today*, is more upfront as regards the status of English as an Indian language. According to Nandy (1973: 8), it is 'a language of our own, yes, an Indian language, in which we could feel deeply, create and convey experiences and responses typically Indian'.

However, whether the Indian writer 'could feel deeply, create and convey experiences and responses typically Indian' is debatable. Rao, for example, in spite of saying that 'English is not really an alien language to us' and that it is 'the language of our *intellectual* make up' has to concede that it is not a language 'of our *emotional* make-up' (author's emphases). Furthermore, it has been noted by Daruwalla (1980) that there are 'handicaps under which an Indian writer, especially a poet, has to labour when writing in English'. Among the handicaps is the poet's difficulty in forging 'a personal language' because 'English never became the language of the common man' but 'remained the language of a vast, unimaginative, colourless bureaucracy that sat like an enormous toad over colonial India' (Daruwalla 1980).

With the tremendous development of Indian literature in English towards the end of the twentieth century, it is arguable whether English continues to be a language that is not of the Indian 'emotional make-up', or whether the Anglo-Indian writer continues to face difficulty in forging 'a personal language'. However, Rao, Narayan and Nandy may have a vested interest in the English language, as Rao and Narayan wrote creatively in the language, and Nandy was the compiler of an anthology of Indian poetry in English. It must also be noted that English at the time of Indian independence from British rule in 1947 was declared only as an 'associate' official language, 'with the expectation', in Walder's words (1998: 90), 'that it would die out within two decades'.

There are also many other Indian commentators who are forthright in their view that English should not be regarded as an Indian language. According to B. Rajan, English is 'a language imposed upon India rather than nourished by its soil' (1974: 79). In contrast, there are at least fifteen major native Indian languages that can be described as being 'nourished by its soil'. Consequently, the justification for writing in English becomes an ongoing dilemma in the history of Indian writing in English. As pointed out by Ashcroft *et al.* (1989: 122–3):

> The problem for critics of Indian writing in English has been that much of their energy has had to go into defending and justifying the decisions of these authors to write in english [sic] at all.

However, it is suggested by the critics that 'they had a more 'authentic' choice of their vernacular language available.

In this regard, B. Rajan (1974: 79) has in fact described Indian literature in English as having 'at least one distinguishing characteristic: its right to be a literature at all is insistently and acrimoniously questioned'.

However, even if the 'national function' of writing in English 'is often questioned and there have been repeated predictions of its demise', the literature, according to King (1974: 14) 'continues to flourish in India'. King's observation was made in 1974. It could be said that, by then, authors of an earlier generation, particularly Narayan, Anand and Rao, had become established figures, and through them 'linguistically speaking, the process of the Indianization of English has acquired an institutional status' (Kachru 1986: 11). In fact, as noted above, Narayan himself proclaims that English 'is now undergoing a process of Indianization'. King's observation that literature in English 'continues to flourish in India' is even truer at the turn of the century with authors such as Vikram Seth and Arundhati Roy, who write novels that are read across the English-speaking world.

The Caribbean

English can be described as the first language of many in the former British colonies of the Caribbean. The novelist George Lamming (1992: 44), in describing his novels, asserts that 'The language in which these books are written is English – which I must repeat – is a West Indian language'. So the kind of soul-searching that confronts anyone who uses the language is not as intense as in other countries or regions. However, this does not mean that the language is fully accepted as it is. The Trinidad-born author, V.S. Naipaul (1972: 26), for example, in a statement which recalls that made by Rao, says that the 'English language was mine; the tradition was not'. Although the 'language was ours to use as we pleased', the literature 'that comes with it was like an alien mythology' to Naipaul (1972: 23). In using the language, 'it seemed impossible' to him 'that the life I knew in Trinidad could ever be turned into a book' (Naipaul 1972: 25).

In order to accommodate English within the Caribbean experience, some writers in the language have resorted to what the poet Edward Kamau Brathwaite has called *nation language*. In Brathwaite's definition, which was given in the previous chapter, a *nation language* is based, but not totally dependent, on a distinctive language, dialect or creole widely spoken in a Caribbean country or by a significant number of its people.

However, Brathwaite (1984:13) refuses to use the word 'dialect' in relation to *nation language*, because 'it carries very pejorative overtones'. Its negative overtones in Caribbean English can be seen, for example, in the aesthetic downgrading, some time ago, of the work of the Jamaican poet Louise Bennett, who was described as 'doing dialect' in her poetry (Donnell and Welsh 1996: 12, 209). However, it must be mentioned that the word *dialect* does not carry such overtones when it is used as a linguistic term. Brathwaite's conception of *nation language* may play an important part in the Caribbean writer's conception of his work, as standard British English may be inadequate to his or her purpose. But this does not mean that English has to be completely rejected – certainly not in the Caribbean context. As Brathwaite (1984: 13) explains, 'it is an English which is not the standard, imported, educated English, but that of the submerged, surrealist experience and sensibility, which has always been there and which is now increasingly coming to the surface and influencing the perception of contemporary Caribbean people'.

Brathwaite's practice in his poetry does not, from the linguistic perspective, slavishly follow standard English, but is faithful, although not entirely dependent on the pidgins and creoles found in his community. Transcending linguistic considerations, he gives credit to aesthetic purpose as well. As such, both his pronouncements on language and his practice in the writing of poetry have been influential. Among the younger poets of Caribbean origin, David Dabydeen, for instance, uses a variation of Guyanese creole in many of his poems, as it is 'the language of his childhood' and, as such, contains its 'rhythms and accents' (Walder 1998: 44). Derek Walcott highlights the virtues of *nation language* by contrasting the choice between largely British-based standard English and creole, or a distinctive Caribbean dialect with American English, in the farce *Beef, No Chicken*. What he does is to pit 'the clichéd expressions of the westernised characters against the rich speechifying traditions of the Caribbean in order to suggest that "progress" leads to cultural impoverishment' (Gilbert and Tompkins 1996: 281).

Singapore

In the case of Singapore, whose main Asian languages are distinct from each other and do not belong to the same language group, the choice of English does seem to be natural. English stands as a bridge language between the various ethnic communities, as most people in the country understand the language. However, the use of English is not uncontroversial, especially during the period shortly after independence. Nevertheless, the controversy has been toned down in recent years, since the status of English as a colonial language has progressively receded over the years, and its practical importance as the language of science and commerce becomes more evident. Even so, the use of English for the writing of literary works is still contentious. In this context, it has been argued that, even if English is important for pragmatic reasons, there is no reason to promote its use for cultural purposes, such as for the writing of literary works.

An innocent or restricted choice

The use of English may not always be loaded with political implications. Indeed, the politics may work the other way round, in the sense that the author's native language may be regarded as too sacred for the writing of literary works, and that English is fittingly 'profane' for writing literary works. This is the reason given by the Maori author Witi Ihimaera (Jussawala and Dasenbrock 1992: 231).

Quite often, however, the reason for the choice of English may be more incidental and less tied to negative spiritual reasons. When Amos Tutuola was asked why he chose to write in English instead of Yorùbá, he replied, innocently, '*I saw an advertisement in a magazine asking for manuscripts, and I wrote* The Palm-Wine Drinkard *and sent it to them*' (Fox 1998: 207; emphasis in the original). The Somali author Nuruddin Farah claimed that he started writing in English because the only typewriter available to him was one that allowed him to write that language. In fact, when he wrote his novel *From a Crooked Rib* in 1970, the Somali language was, officially at least, an unwritten language, as the use of the romanised script for writing the language was only officially made available in 1972. However, in 1973 the military regime in Somalia prevented Farah from completing a serialised novel written in Somali, resulting in his being discouraged from writing further in the language.

Indeed, an author may write in English simply because a practical opportunity, or a series of opportunities, presents itself, whereas writing in the author's native tongue, as in the case of Farah, may not only be less practical but is fraught with political hazards. Or the author may personally find English better in relation to the adequacy of expression, description or narration in the writing of his works, as in the case of Raja Rao. Rao finds his own native language Kannada, compared with English, 'never adequate' for the writing of his fiction (Jussawala and Dasenbrock 1992: 144). He also finds languages like Sanskrit and French less flexible than English. However, claims that English is innocently used by chance, that the author is more proficient in it than his or her native language or that it is more flexible than other languages are, arguably, by no means free from politics. In response to all these claims, it can be argued that there are usually more opportunities to write in English than in other languages, and the author should not merely take advantage of them without thinking of the possibility of writing in the native language.

The claim that the author's own native language is inadequate compared with English can be easily exaggerated, as the problem may not lie with the language itself, but with the author's lack of proficiency in his or her language compared with English, as in the case of the Pakistani author of Parsi descent, Bapsi Sidhwa. Sidhwa is frank in her admission of lesser proficiency in what she describes as her first and second languages (Gujerati and Urdu respectively) than in English. To her, 'as far as writing and reading goes, I can read and write best in English', even though she did find when she moved to America that 'all my sentences were punctuated with Gujarati and Urdu words' (in Jussawala and Dasenbrock 1992: 214).

The limitation of choice for some authors may indeed be even more restricted than that open to Sidhwa. Buchi Emecheta, for example, is not able to write stories in her native language Igbo. The problems noted by Achebe in relation to Igbo mentioned in the previous chapter are undoubtedly a contributory factor, as Emecheta is able to write in another Nigerian language, Yorùbá. She, however, prefers to write in English. Yorùbá is the native language of Nigerian writer Wole Soyinka. Interestingly, in Soyinka's autobiographical novel *Aké*, the protagonist as a child responds in English when he is rescued by a white man, even though the white man speaks to him in elementary Yorùbá. Apparently, the protagonist does not even have a command of elementary spoken Yorùbá in order to carry out a conversation with the white man. Although Yorùbá has been described as having 'one of the richest literary traditions of literature in all of Africa' (Westley 1992: 161), Soyinka writes in English because he feels that he is more confident in it.

Moving back to the South Asian sub-continent, the poet Nissim Ezekiel has defended his use of the English language in the following terms: "To write poetry in English because one cannot write it in any other language is surely not a despicable decision' (1969: 170–1). This remark finds an echo in Shashi Deshpande, who said that English 'was the only language I could write' (Dickman 1998: 131). Likewise, Zulfikar Ghose, who was born in Pakistan, has said that 'English is the only language I have'. But this does not seem to pose a problem to Ghose, as he regards himself as British, and 'really more Anglo-Saxon than the Anglo-Saxons' (in Jussawala and Dasenbrock 1992: 187).

Literature in a borrowed tongue

English has been described as a *borrowed tongue*. But the borrowing here does seem to be long term. One wonders if the language will ever be 'returned' to what the character Obi Okonkwo in Achebe's *No Longer At Ease* describes as its 'proud owners'. One person who had the courtesy to want to 'return' the English language to the English was James Joyce. As noted in Chapter 2, Stephen Daedalus, the main character of Joyce's *Portrait of the Artist as a Young Man*, expresses the view that the spoken English of the Dean of Studies 'will always be for me an acquired speech'. With reference to his final novel *Finnegans Wake*, which was described in Chapter 2 as an excellent example of a postcolonial text, Joyce wrote that 'I'll give them back their English language. I'm not destroying it for good' (cited by Ellmann 1982: 546).

In wanting to give them back their language, Joyce is not quite returning it intact, but, to quote Eagleton (1995: 269) again, he estranges 'the English language in the eyes of its proprietors', and 'struck a blow on behalf of all of his gagged and humiliated ancestors'. In the same vein, Achebe has said, with a touch of menace, that African writers intend 'to do unheard of things' with the English language (1975: 9). From a symbolic postcolonial angle, the former imperial masters, as the 'custodians' of the language in England – where 'real or proper English' is to be found, and where it is 'preserved, and listed like a property of the National Trust' (Widdowson 1994: 377) – might not be happy that their language is 'returned' to them in such a state by Irishmen, Africans and others.

In wanting to return their language to the English, Joyce was of course being ironic. However, he does suggest the fact that the act of borrowing is unusual in at least two irreconcilable respects: that the language may retain more of its original characteristics when it is used by the borrower, or – as is more commonly the case perhaps – it no longer retains many of its original native characteristics. The former is seen in Joyce's *Portrait*, where, with reference to a frequently cited event in the novel, the original meaning of the word 'tundish' is retained in Ireland, but not in England. Stephen finds the word 'English and good old blunt English too' and questions the Dean's motive in teaching him English later in the novel: 'What did he come here for to teach us his own language or to learn it from us.' (1960: 256).

Examples in which the English language no longer retains its original native characteristics after being 'borrowed' are more plentiful. The Singaporean writer of fiction Catherine Lim, for instance, has said that:

> The way I write is not the same as the way a native speaker would write. I am influenced by Hokkien [a Chinese language], where the rhythm is different, and I use local words.
>
> (Mangan 1998: 7)

The English language used may indeed become so different from the language as it is spoken in England that it becomes less of a borrowed tongue, because its relationship to English in the country of its native origin has become tenuous.

As noted earlier, the original 'owners' of English have 'loaned' it – or, indeed, have given it away – to so many other people that they have in effect ceased to become its unique owners. Moreover, something very different from the attempt to make English distinct from the original language can happen. This 'borrowed tongue' – if it can continue to be described as such – is so entrenched in the culture of many of the 'borrowers' that they can become more proficient in it than the 'lenders'. In spite of its designation as a 'borrowed tongue', it may even attain the status of a national language, if its general level of proficiency is high, as is the case in Ghana. In this regard, it has been noted in the *Ghanaian Independent* that although 'Our national language is a borrowed tongue', the students of Achimota School in Ghana 'rattle English I dare say better than some typical backyard public schools in hinterland Britain' ('Are We Serious about Culture?').

However, the status of English as an official or even national language in Africa is not left unchallenged, as seen earlier in this chapter. It needs to be noted that it faces opposition, for example, from an expected quarter – Ngũgĩ, who views it in terms of the influential position of the middle classes in Africa. The high status of English in Ghana, which had the longest history of British colonial rule in West Africa, is occasionally questioned within the country (Quarcoo 1994: 329, 331). According to Ngũgĩ, the promotion of English in Africa is reflective 'of the willful narcissism ... of the African middle class, which sees itself as constituting the nation'. Since 'they constitute the nation, it makes logical sense [to them] that the languages they speak and use [such as English] are the ones which are truly national' (Ngũgĩ 1998: 93).

Literature of one's own and pedagogy

Although written in the English language, literatures can be and have been regarded by the non-English peoples writing it as 'a literature of one's own'. In the words of the Indian writer Raja Rao (1963: vii), in the foreword to his novel *Kanthapura*, 'One has to convey in a language that is not one's own a spirit that is one's own'. In this respect, the literature they write, because it differs, among other things, in its spirit, is distinct from literatures in English written in England and in other countries or geopolitical regions. The texts they have written thus have a unique identity and are similar in certain respects to other works that come from the same area, even if they are written in other languages. They are also different from those originating in other areas.

Mining the rich fields of one's tradition

One very important reason why such literatures appear distinct is that the writers have mined their own traditions to write their works. As noted above, it is at times difficult to distinguish local influences from the English and European ones. Some authors, in writing their works in English, have made a conscious attempt to make use of their national, ethnic or religious myths, beliefs, aesthetic outlook, philosophy and even language. The influence of local tradition or sensibility on a literary work may sometimes be subtle, and hence creates further difficulties in distinguishing local and foreign influences.

Mining the author's traditions has its pitfalls, one of which is the possible failure to communicate with people who do not come from the same background as the author. Although this may not be a problem if authors want to communicate only with their own people, this is not the case with many of the writers today. They would like to have a wider general audience, which the English language allows them to have. Many of them have managed to mine their own traditions while securing a wide audience for their works.

In looking for one's tradition, there is always the danger that the author has to invent a pseudo-tradition in order to make the literary work distinctive. Soyinka (1975) has described this as Neo-Tarzanism (see also Ashcroft *et al.*'s comments 1989: 128–130). However, the idea of 'inventing tradition' is more widespread, and what can be regarded as 'traditional' is quite often re-created, or 'invented'. For example, the nationalist ideology advocated by Gandhi 'sought to define and fix what were thought to be indigenous, precolonial cultural models' (Lelyveld 1993: 191).

Literature and pedagogy

Even in the white settler colonies, the use of their own literatures in the English language curriculum is beset with problems. Some of the problems have to do with national identity, whereby the literatures of the white settler colonies – many of whose texts explore questions of identities that are distinct from a British or English identity – need to be taught in school or university, but are not found in the curriculum. The situation beyond the white settler colonies is not significantly different. If anything, it may actually be stronger. Achebe (1975: 19), for example, has declared that 'art for art's sake is just another piece of deodorised dog-shit'. Achebe believes that there is a powerful link between literature and education as conceived in a broad sense.

One of the significant figures who tried to change the literature curriculum in African schools and universities by including more African literary works was Ngũgĩ. In 1968, he and his colleagues at the University of Nairobi produced a document which tried to conceive what has been desscribed as 'the constitution of African literary study as a legitimate academic discipline with certified degrees and professional specialization' (Jehyo 1990: 43). However, as mentioned earlier, Ngũgĩ has problems with African literature written in English. There are thus always qualifications that are pushed to the foreground whenever one proposes the use of literature in English for education, even with regard to texts that may have a part to play in the development of national consciousness.

6   Decolonisation and the survival of English

After achieving independence – which occurred at a rapid pace after the Second World War – the former colonies of Britain questioned the continued use of the English language. According to Ngũgĩ 'the language issue is a very important key to the decolonization process' (Jussawala and Dasenbrock 1992: 30). However, the approaches to the continued use of English in the colonies, as we have seen in the previous chapter, were not uniform, and there were clear differences between them. An important question underlying the different approaches was whether English was spoken by the population as a native language or whether it was a language imposed on them.

For the white settler colonies where English is spoken as a native language, such as Australia and Canada, its continued use was never seriously questioned by the more politically powerful white settlers, even if its use was at the expense of the indigenous languages. The indigenous population, however, did not have sufficient political clout to ensure that their languages be promoted or at least preserved. Many of the Aboriginal languages of Australia, as noted earlier, have become extinct. In Canada, in addition to the fear that English threatened the survival of the native languages, there was the fear that English might overwhelm French.

Beyond the settler colonies, independence more naturally led to a questioning of the position of English. However, the intensity of questioning varied according to the ethnic and linguistic composition of each community. In general, if there was more heterogeneity of the racial and linguistic composition of the state, it was likely that English would continue to play a part. However, if there was homogeneity, or if one racial or linguistic group was dominant or formed the majority, then the continued use of English was questioned, and the language of the majority or the dominant community would replace English.

Another important consideration is history. Looking at this as a factor, an even more rigid divide than that between West and East Africa, which was mentioned in the previous chapter, can be seen if the whole of anglophone Africa is compared with the Caribbean. Philip Sherlock, for example, has noted that 'Colonialism, however important, was an incident in the history of Nigeria and Ghana, Kenya or Uganda; but it is the whole history of the West Indies' and, as such, 'has a deeper meaning for the West Indian than for the African' (1966: 13–14). British colonialism quite naturally led, owing to its overwhelming presence in the history of the West Indies, to the retention of English.

Continued colonisation with English?

It has been argued that it is through the continued use of the English language, and the values encoded in it, that British colonialism is perpetuated. But it is a subtler kind of colonialism that is sustained after independence, for it now lives, virtually unnoticed, in the minds of the native population. In an earlier era, English education, as argued by Viswanathan (1989), was the means by which British power was assigned to a native elite who merely acted as British surrogates. These surrogates for British rule continue to sustain a more elusive form of British colonialism after independence.

The psychological basis of whether the countries continue to be colonised after the British have left can be questioned here. Gandhi was an example of a leader who believed that psychological colonialism would continue, even after the physical withdrawal of the colonisers. He argued, before leaving South Africa for India, that freedom without the rejection of English was tantamount to 'English rule without the Englishman' (cited by Lelyveld 1993: 190). He believed that only an Indian language could reach 'the heart of the nation' (Lelyveld 1993: 189, 191). However, it must be mentioned that Gandhi's view on this matter was not limited to language, but to the rejection of modern technology as well, which he regards as 'Western' or 'English'. There is thus a conflation of the modern and the Western, with the English language somehow thrown into the picture.

Neutrality of English?

In multilingual postcolonial societies, such as Nigeria, Zambia and Singapore, English is quite often regarded as a neutral language. If there is a single native language in a country, or a particular 'neutral' local language is widely used as a lingua franca, it is easy to argue against the continued use of English. But where no single language is dominant in a multilingual society, as in the three countries mentioned above, English can be used as a bridge language.

Braj Kachru (1986: 8–9) notes the neutrality of English in the postcolonial Indian context:

> English does have one clear advantage, attitudinally and linguistically: it has acquired a *neutrality* in a linguistic context where native languages, dialects and styles sometimes have acquired undesirable connotations. Whereas native codes are functionally marked in terms of caste, religion, region, and so forth, English has no such 'markers', at least in the non-native context.

Indeed, in the Indian context, English may not only be perceived as a neutral language, but may serve a peacemaking role, as suggested by the character Aurora Zogoiby in Salman Rushdie's *The Moor's Last Sigh* (1995: 179):

> It was at this time, when language riots prefigured the division of the state, that she announced that neither Marathi nor Gujarati would be spoken within her walls; the language of her kingdom was English and nothing but. All these different lingos cuttofy us off from one another,' she explained. 'Only English brings us together.'

Aurora's use of the neologism 'cuttofy' appears to be a blend of the word 'cut' and the '-fy' suffix, which makes it resemble the word 'unify'. It thus places it more noticeably as the antonym of the word 'unify', which suggests that a language such as Marathi or Gujarati is the opposite of a unifying language. The use of the word 'lingo' must also be mentioned, for it is defined by the *Oxford English Dictionary* as 'A contemptuous designation for: Foreign speech or language; language which is strange or unintelligible to the person who so designates it', which perhaps indicates Aurora's own personal view of Marathi and Gujerati when contrasted to English.

In this light, not only has England ceased to be the colonial power, but the status of the language that it disseminated via colonialism has also changed. English is now less often viewed negatively, as it has the practical advantage of uniting diverse multilingual communities together. It can thus be argued that English today is no longer the language of colonialism. However, this view is debatable, and various counter-arguments have already been presented in this book.

English as a channel of nationalistic anti-colonialism

Nevertheless, even if English remains the language of colonialism, it is easy to argue against the view that British colonisation *per se* remains with the continued use of the language. It has been said, for example, that writers who use English 'are using the primary tool of oppression as a means of their own liberation' (Baker 2000: 274). In the same vein, Salman Rushdie claims that 'To conquer English may be to complete the process of making ourselves free' (1991: 17). It has also been maintained that by the wider usage of English, it is the English language itself that has been decolonised, as it naturally becomes less closely associated with the former colonial power. English has in fact been used, in various ways, as a tool to effectively attack Britain as a colonial power. Achebe's claim that he chose to learn English and to write in it in order to infiltrate 'the ranks of the enemy' and to destroy 'him from within' is not his only statement on the use of English for anti-colonialism. He has said elsewhere that 'we needed [the British's] language to transact our business, including the business of overthrowing colonialism itself in the fulness of time' (quoted by Brückner 1996: 77). According to the South African writer Es'kia Mphahlele, English (like French) has become 'the common language with which to present a nationalist front against the white oppressors', and even 'where the whiteman has already retreated, as in the independent states' English is 'still a unifying force' (paraphrased by Ngũgĩ 1986: 7).

In an earlier study, Ali Mazrui (1966) points out that much of the liberation struggle against British colonialism in Africa is carried out via English, and not through African languages. Although this may be regarded as natural, especially if the focus is restricted to British colonies, Mazrui also believes, like Mphahlele, that English serves a nation-building function, which can be particularly constructive in postcolonial contexts. In another study, Mazrui (1975) points out that where English is used as a lingua franca in Africa, a transcendent national consciousness that goes beyond the confines of individual tribes becomes possible. In this regard, the de-emphasis of traditional beliefs, and of tribal connections which came about through the use of English, gave rise to detribalization, which in turn made possible the kind of nationalism that opposed British colonial rule. Moreover, Mazrui explains that the use of English gave rise to a consolidating impetus among African nations using the language, which resulted in the development of extra-national anti-colonial movements such as Pan-Africanism and Pan-Negroism.

However, the importance of English in the anti-colonial struggle must be qualified. Looking at the language, not everyone agrees that it is English *per se* that is revolutionary. According to Brathwaite (1984: 13), '*It is not language, but people, who make revolutions*' (Brathwaite's emphasis). Others, such as Ngũgĩ, are forthright that English should not be used at all in the anti-colonial struggle. He gives his view (Ngũgĩ 1986: 28) on why he arrives at the decision to write in Gĩkũyũ:

> I believe that my writing in Gĩkũyũ language, a Kenyan language, an African language, is part and parcel of the anti-imperialist struggles of Kenyan and African peoples. In schools and universities our Kenyan languages – that is the languages of the many nationalities which make up Kenya – were associated with negative qualities of backwardness, under-development, humiliation and punishment.

It is interesting to contrast Ngũgĩ's view with that of Mazrui above, both of whom originated in East Africa but clearly have differing views on the matter. The contrast also makes the division between East and West Africa, with regard to the attitude towards English, not an unqualified one, as the East African stance on the matter is not homogeneous.

English as a world language

For good or ill, one has to contend with the importance of English as a world language (for more recent discussions, see Crystal 1997 and Graddol 1996). Knowledge of the language is helpful for career advancement or widening the learning of many disciplines. It is the kind of knowledge that many people today cannot afford to be without. These are undoubtedly positive aspects of knowing English, even if the language itself has been imposed, at least in its initial stages, through dubious means. Some of these positive aspects will be discussed below. However, there are also some negative aspects which need to be highlighted later in this chapter.

Does English still belong to the English?

As a result of its rise as a world language, the English language, as noted earlier, no longer 'belongs' to the English. In the words of T.J. Cribb (1999: 119), 'It belongs to everybody who can gain access and is owned by no one'. This argument could be carried a step further, by asking whether the language should continue to be called 'English', which is indeed the question asked by the Australian poet A.D. Hope (1989: 21), 'should we not find a new name for a language which no longer belongs to England any more than to Scotland or India or Australia or the United States?'

Practical value of English

English today is not only the language of science and technology but also the language of commerce and the Internet. In India, for example, Dennis Walder has noted that the 'demands of global economics and technology [have] proved irresistible' to the middle classes (Walder 1998: 90). Although Hindi is the national language of India, English has also become, in addition to Hindi, a means for the attainment of national unity. According to Walder (1998; 90) English in India, as 'a vital medium of communication', is 'a means of keeping people together'. Thus it is easier for creative writing in the language to thrive with a pragmatic basis underlying its use.

A similar situation to that seen in India is found in many African countries, where, in Achebe's words, 'There are not many countries ... today where you could abolish the language of the erstwhile colonial masters and still retain the facility for mutual communication' (1965: 28). The importance of English is such that Achebe (1965: 28) even suggests that 'the national literature of Nigeria and of many other African countries of Africa is, or will be, written in English'.

English is thus an important language for national development. It is not only India and Nigeria that recognise this. Even countries not colonised by Britain are learning English and are teaching the language to their young, although it is unlikely that these countries will produce literature in the language as vibrant as that found among writers of Indian or Nigerian origin.

English and its cultural baggage

Although a practical linguistic base is beneficial for the growth of literature in the language, this does not mean that this base alone is sufficient to ensure its growth. In fact, there are many people, who wish that the use of English remains at the practical level and does not rise up to high culture (Talib 1994: 155–6). This attitude is especially prevalent in countries that have quite recently gained independence from Britain, but, in some cases, it remains long after independence. So long as English is used for practical purposes, the learning of the language is not controversial. However, using the language for the writing of literature means that it is used for cultural reasons, and its use thus becomes more contentious. In this light, its use for popular culture is seen as less harmful. The singing of pop songs in English, for example, is rather frequently seen today as an innocent activity, although there are exceptions to this, as seen in the French government's attempt to control radio broadcasts of popular songs in English (Sage 1996).

In relation to the negative attitude towards the use of English for literature, even a defender of the language such as Achebe (1965: 28) recognises that English 'came as part of a package deal which included many other items of doubtful value and the positive atrocity of racial arrogance and prejudice which may yet set the world on fire'. It must also be mentioned that in most cases, although English is the language of government and commerce, it is not spoken with any degree of fluency by the majority of the population, thus alienating most of the people from the state and its formal sectors (Olaniyan 2000). Ngũgĩ, as we have seen, goes one step further by stating his belief that not only must the negative aspects or tendencies associated with the use of English be acknowledged, but action must be taken against its continued use. To him, 'decolonisation' means the voluntary extraction from European values and world view, which are inevitably activated when English is used. Thus the way out is the avoidance of the use of English for high culture, which was what Ngũgĩ eventually did in relation to his creative writing.

The survival/flowering of literature

In many countries, literature in English not only 'survives' after decolonisation, but it can be said that the real and substantial beginning of the literature takes place only after decolonisation. This is the case with Singaporean literature in English, which for several reasons, only grew after independence (Talib 1998: 271). In relation to Indian poetry in English, R. Parthasarathy (1976: 3) has noted that 'one comes up, first of all, with the paradox that it did not seriously begin to exist till after the withdrawal of the British from India'. This is also seen as a paradox by N.A. Karim (1998), who has commented more generally on Indian literature in the language:

> It is a little surprising that the number of Indian writers in English both creative and otherwise, has increased phenomenally after the English left the country. During the colonial period, English was

being nurtured as a potted plant with no freedom for this tongue to take roots in the socio-cultural soil of the country. Speakers and writers of the language generally tried to conform to the standard of English spoken and written by their masters in England in matters of grammar, vocabulary and even pronunciation. This self-imposed constraint made the medium inflexible for any meaningful creative effort. But after the British left, Indians began to take greater freedom with the language and began shaping it into an effective instrument to give expression to their native experience.

It is not only literature in English which blossoms, but, as Raja Rao claims, the English language itself has shown an improvement in its standard of usage in India and has become more suitable for local situations. According to Rao (in Jussawala and Dasenbrock 1992: 149):

> The English we use in India today is a much better English than it was some forty to fifty years ago ... Most of the English I read in magazines in India today is very much better indeed ... English in India is so much more interesting and much freer than it used to be.

There was however the belief, at one point, that both the English language and literature in the language in India had declined. This belief was based on the lack of Indian creative writers with works to match the quality of work produced by writers born in the first decade of the twentieth century, such as Narayan, Anand and Rao himself. But this has changed with the emergence of major works in English from writers of Indian origin in the last two decades of the century. The major work that started the ball rolling here was Salman Rushdie's *Midnight's Children*, which according to Anita Desai 'seemed to set tongues free in India in an odd way' (Jussawala and Dasenbrock 1992: 172).

It was not only Indian literature in English which flowered after independence, as the growth could also be seen, according to Alamgir Hashmi and Malashri Lal (1998: 7), across the sub-continent:

> ... the phenomenal rise in both quantity and quality of writing in English in all forms is evidently the most significant cultural aspect of the postindependence era – all the more striking as it has happened in certain instances contrary to expectation, and even declared government policy, and not just in Pakistan or India, but also in Sri Lanka and Bangladesh.

Often it not so much a flourishing of literature in English that can be noticed after independence but that its significance emerges only then. At a more global level, Bruce King (1992) has noted that modern drama in English in the Commonwealth only began between 1950 and 1965, which was roughly the period of political and cultural decolonisation. Moving beyond drama, Jussawala and Dasenbrock (1992: 4) have made the general observation that 'with a very few exceptions significant writing in English from the former colonies dates not from the colonial but from the post-colonial period'.

Wider audience with English

One advantage in using English is that writers can attain a larger audience. Anuki, the native language of the Papua New Guinean novelist Russell Soaba, has fewer than 300 speakers, and it is natural for him to choose English in order to gain a wider audience. Indeed, in Soaba's case, it is not paradoxical to say that he chose English out of 'choicelessness' (cited by Skinner 1998: 127). But English is also chosen by authors whose native language has many more speakers. In the Nigerian context, D.S. Izevbaye has noted that English serves the function of gaining 'for Nigerian literature a much wider audience than is available to the older vernacular literatures in, for example, Hausa and Yoruba' (1974: 137). The Nigerian author Zaynab Alkali, for example – whose first language is Hausa – has acknowledged that she would naturally 'feel more comfortable writing in my own language but the audience, as you know, would be limited' (James 1990: 31).

Although Ngũgĩ is a prominent example of a postcolonial writer who has abandoned English for creative writing in favour of his native language Gĩkũyũ, not many writers can follow his example. It has been noted by John Skinner, for example, that a younger, less established writer than Ngũgĩ could not have followed his example without losing a great deal. Skinner (1998: 105) explains that it 'might have been more economically damaging for a younger writer who had not yet found an audience', and who 'would also have passed unnoticed among the international literary community' to reject English if he or she is proficient in writing in the language creatively.

Moreover, no sub-Saharan African language has as large an audience in the continent as European languages such as English and French, except perhaps for Kiswahili, which is widely spoken in Central and Eastern Africa. The case of Kiswahili has prompted Wole Soyinka to suggest that it should be a pan-African language and the literary language used by African writers (Soyinka 1976; Wilkinson 1992: 94–

5). Soyinka is, incidentally, not from Eastern Africa but from Nigeria in West Africa, and not a speaker of Kiswahili (for another West African perspective on the use of Kiswahili as a lingua franca, see Okonkwo 1976; 1979: 103). Interestingly, when Ngũgĩ decided to turn away from English, he chose his native language Gĩkũyũ, and not Kiswahili, which could have earned him a wider audience able to read his works in its original language.

Ironically, some of Ngũgĩ's works in Gĩkũyũ have been banned in Kenya, thus restricting his audience even further. In spite of the ban, Ngũgĩ has defended his continued use of Gĩkũyũ by saying that 'If there are such strong reactions from the government, then writing in Gĩkũyũ must be doing something which writing in English does not do' (Jussawala and Dasenbrock 1992: 28). It should also be added that Ngũgĩ has been exiled for many years from Kenya, which also means that he has been separated from the Gĩkũyũ-speaking community. However, Ngũgĩ's reputation was well established before he made the decision to stop using English for his creative works, whereas for the younger writers, especially if they were to face some of the obstacles that Ngũgĩ faced, it would be a futile endeavour.

Differences between countries

There are undoubted differences in the attitude towards English between countries. Where there is a single native language in a country, or a particular 'neutral' language is widely used as a lingua franca, it is easy to argue against the continued use of English. However, in a multilingual society where no single language is dominant, and where it may be politically dangerous for a particular local language to be used at the expense of other languages, English can be used as a bridge language. For example, D. S. Izevbaye has described English in Nigeria as providing 'a basis for a national literature by creating a meeting point for the country's cultural diversity' (1974: 137).

It must be stated here that the principle that English can be used as a bridge language in a multilingual state which does not have a single dominant local language does not apply across the board. India, for example, is a multilingual country, but, as noted above, Gandhi had advocated that English should be rejected, and Gandhi's call was endorsed as a goal during the struggle for independence. However, looking for a national language for India was not an easy task. Hindi or Hindustani was not the language spoken by all Indians, and, in fact, is still not universally understood throughout India today, especially in areas of Southern India where Dravidian languages such as Tamil and

Telugu are spoken. Gandhi himself was not initially conversant in Hindi or Hindustani, but took the trouble to learn it. It was mentioned, for example, that during one of his campaigns, he spent 'every spare moment, at meals and even in the lavatory, studying a Hindustani primer' (Lelyveld 1993: 192).

Arguably, most countries are multilingual, and so, at least in theory, English, as a neutral language, should be allowed to survive by the ruling political elite. But the real situation is certainly not as simple as this, and even if English is allowed to thrive in a multilingual society, this does not mean that good literature in the language will be produced. Moreover, not all countries have a developed tradition of literary writings in English, which is important, although not necessary, for the continued growth of literature in the language.

Cultural imperialism: English edging out other cultures

In spite of many positive qualities in the continued use of English, all is not rosy with its global dominance in the world today. One of the criticisms levelled against global English is that it is guilty of *cultural imperialism*, as it has a tendency to sideline other languages. Although, as mentioned in Chapter 3, it may be American cultural imperialism that is ultimately at work here, there is no question that it is the English language that has benefited from American dominance. At the same time however, cultural imperialism may not be entirely American, nor, as pointed out in Chapter 3, is it wholly linguistic. Indeed, it is often combined with other non-linguistic or semi-linguistic aspects of culture, although it is difficult to determine where linguistically based cultural imperialism begins, and where it ends. In Ghana, for example, where English is the national language:

> Our Ministers of State go to work in three piece suits, and we give English names to our children. Go to a State Banquet at the Banquet Hall, or attend a function at the National Theatre – you will see the McKwesi Kyei Darkwa dressed as if attending dinner at Buckingham Palace.
>
> We have reduced culture to "drumming and dancing", a preserve of adolescent dancing groups, dotted in the city.
>
> ('Are We Serious About Culture?')

Literature in English edging out other literatures

Another manifestation of cultural imperialism occurs when literature in English causes a decline in the other literatures, or edges them out by diverting attention away from them. Some aspects of this issue were discussed in Chapter 4, especially in relation to the sidelining of oral literature in native languages. A further example of this tendency is represented by *The Vintage Book of Indian Writing 1947–1997*, co-edited by Salman Rushdie, which includes only works written in English. Rushdie justifies his restriction by saying that Indian writing in English is 'proving to be a stronger and more important body of work than most of what has been produced in the official languages of India' (Rushdie 1997a: x).

Many people will find it difficult to agree with Rushdie's view. However, except for the written languages in Bengali, the Southern Indian Dravidian languages such as Tamil and Malayalam, and, arguably, Hindi and Urdu the written versions of the other languages of India developed late. Even in the case of written Hindi and Urdu, their more complete development largely occurred in the nineteenth century, when Indian literature started to be written in English. For many Indian languages, it was only in the nineteenth century that a written script began to be used. Thus written literature in most Indian languages did not have sufficient time to mature.

Written literature in English thus has as lengthy a history in India as many of the written literatures in the indigenous languages. In fact, some of the best authors in English today are Indian or of Indian descent, hence indicating how important they are, not only within India itself but worldwide. Their global importance is such that the acrimonious debate of the fifties and sixties – when defenders of writing in English 'fought out a national, even nationalistic, battle' with defenders of literary writing in Indian languages – has receded, and the writers in English have become 'models for Indian-language writers' (Dharwadker and Dharwadker 1996: 92, 94). Nevertheless, it is not difficult to see that the growth of Indian literature in English may be at the expense of literatures in the indigenous Indian languages.

Literature written in English, with its long history extending beyond India itself, should not only be compared with literatures written in the Indian languages, many of whose written scripts were introduced much later. The oral literary tradition of many of the Indian languages, just as much as the oral literary tradition of African languages, should also be considered.

In general, it can be noted that the development of literature in English has taken critical and scholarly attention away, relatively speaking, from literature in the indigenous languages. The multilingual literatures of a particular country have become dominant in their own right, even though they have not been written in the original languages of the country. In the case of India, the literatures in the other languages need not be of low quantity and quality, or show a decline in quality, for this diversion of attention to take place.

With reference to African literature, Karin Barber (1999: 125) has noted that:

> The 'postcolonial' criticism of the 1980s and 1990s ... has promoted a binarized, generalized model of the world which has had the effect of eliminating African-language expression from view. This model has produced an impoverished and distorted picture of 'the colonial experience' and the place of language in that experience.

Barber further elaborates that:

> ... this model blocks a properly historical, localized understanding of any scene of colonial and post-Independence literary production in Africa. Instead it selects and overemphasizes one sliver of literary and cultural production – written literature in the English language – and treats this as all there is, representative of a whole culture or even a global 'colonial experience'. It thus negligently or deliberately erases all other forms of expression – written literature in African languages, oral literature in African languages, and a whole domain of cultural forms which cross the boundaries between 'written' and 'oral', between 'foreign' and 'indigenous'...

Instead of helping literatures written in the indigenous languages, literatures in English, whether in India or Africa, seem to have caused their neglect.

Quite clearly, although the old form of imperialism might have ended in many parts of the world, the new form of imperialism, whereby English plays a dominating role, is still with us. This new imperialism, aided by American economic and political power, has become stronger over the years, partly because of the continued dominance of English and the strength of the United States as its primary sponsor. Those who speak and write in English – comfortable as they are with the importance of the language – should treat its worldwide dominance with some concern. The world will be a poorer place to live in should the other languages and their associated cultures simply disappear, or become enfeebled as a consequence of the rise of English, abetted by continuing American supremacy in the cultural sphere.

7 Style, language(s), politics and acceptability

The style of world English literatures

In a way, the study of the style of world English literatures is not different from the study of style in more mainstream British or American literature. Some of the stylistic features found in mainstream literature can thus be observed in them. However, studying these features will not make world English literatures distinctive when compared with mainstream literature. In this case, studying them might as well be carried out in a book that does not make a distinction between mainstream and world English literatures.

There are indeed features that are striking, especially if the language used differs significantly from standard British English. However, the differences in the linguistic features may depend on the categories that they belong to. In this light, Kirsten Malmkjær (1999: 89–90) has observed that 'though variance is warmly welcomed by the sound system, and generously allowed for in the lexis, it seems to be fiercely resisted by grammar'. The scope for variation in grammar thus seems to be more limited when compared with variations in pronunciation and vocabulary, although there are some significant exceptions. It does seem to be the case, therefore, that, unless the exceptions are analysed, it is usually more fruitful to look for variation at the levels of phonology and lexis than at the level of grammar. Indeed, if there is significant variation in grammar, it can be argued that what is analysed might not be a dialect of English, but a pidgin or creole (these terms will be explained later in this chapter).

It must be mentioned at the onset that although the use of Englishes that deviate from standard British English is the main concern in this chapter, it does not mean that all authors make an insistent attempt to use it. R.K. Narayan, to pick a prominent example, largely uses language that does not differ very much from standard British English in his works, although he claims, as seen in Chapter 5, that English in India has undergone 'a process of Indianization'. Indeed, according to Alastair Niven, 'I think it would be hard to find a more fastidious use of English than in Narayan' (Ramnarayan 2000). For example, in the following extract from his novel *The Painter of Signs* (Narayan 1978: 91), although there is reference to the Hindu concept of reincarnation, the grammar and syntax are not reflective of a distinctive variety of Indian English:

> 'I feel as if we had known each other several Janmas,' he said rather plaintively.
>   'It is imagination really' she said. 'Do you believe in reincarnation?'

In the above, which is quite representative of Narayan's language use in his works, the language is pretty much standard English, although the concept of reincarnation and the Sanskrit word *Janma* (which can be understood to mean lifetime) are used.

In general, the examples of dialect or other non-standard uses, although common enough in world English literatures, are not universally found in all works. In fact, there is a general tendency not to resort to non-standard usage, and some of the reasons have been mentioned in the introduction to N.F. Blake's *Non-Standard Language in English Literature* (1981: 11–20). An important reason mentioned by Blake is the inability of readers to understand the non-standard English used in the work. Although Blake's book is largely on literature from Britain, his observation can also be carried over to the other literatures in English, many of whose authors avoid using non-standard English for fear that their works will not get a wide readership.

Availability and use of dialects of English or other languages

Although the use of English dialects in literary works is usually not purely inventive but based on actual spoken dialects, elements of imaginative recreation, or borrowings from earlier writers, can be found, and are a common practice in mainstream literature. As dialects can be found in quite a number of works in mainstream literature, writers could simply learn how to use them from earlier writers. Edmund Spenser, for example, was believed not to have used dialects that existed during his time of writing, but to have borrowed them from earlier writers. However, the possibility of simply learning dialect usage from earlier writers may plainly not be available for literatures outside the mainstream, especially if the literatures are in their early stages of development.

The depiction of actual language use may come naturally to some writers. Other writers, however, may go to great lengths to get as accurate a representation of language as possible in their works. For example, the South African writer Essop Patel is of the view that he has 'to listen to people, walking around with a tape recorder on street corners and recording their conversation'. In spite of Essop's efforts, the difficulty, according to him, of attempting 'to transcribe people's patois with the correct diction' remains (Wilkinson 1992: 171).

Thus a dialect in a literary work may need to represent, to a certain extent, some of its conspicuous peculiarities and not merely to ignore them completely, even if comprehensibility to non-speakers may not be totally attained. For example, the dominant dialect of English spoken in Jamaica has a distinct syntax of its own. The Jamaican writer who wants to depict the dialect must therefore try to represent its syntax, even if it varies significantly from standard British English. In general, significant deviations in syntax may result in the language used being regarded as a pidgin or creole, and not merely a dialect of English. This may very well be the case with the more distinctive varieties of Jamaican English, which, of course, when they are used in a literary work, may affect the reach of its readership. However, the Jamaican writer has a range of linguistic *levels*, ranging from standard Jamaican English (much of which is globally comprehensible), to a Jamaican dialect of English, to creole (which is not comprehensible to other speakers of English). According to Louis James (2000: 120–1), citing an example given by David Lawton (1980), 'a Jamaican may say to a European, "it is my father's car"; to an acquaintance, "it is mi faadaz kyaar'; and to an intimate, "di kyaar a fi me faada" '. The language used in the church, for example, especially if the church official wants to give friendly advice to a churchgoer, is likely to be in the middle of the range. Here is an illustration from Michelle Cliff's *No Telephone to Heaven* (1987: 37) (the addressee is a boy named Christopher), which uses a distinct variety of Jamaican English:

> You is one lucky bwai to have such a name. It mean … you name mean the bearer of Christ. Children, dis here bwai is name bearer of Christ … him who bring Lickle Jesus into de New World. Into our world. T'ink 'pon dese t'ings. Christ come wid Columbus.
>
> [Ellipses in the original]

The above is quite easily understood, in spite of some grammatical deviations from standard English, such as the lack of number concord and past tense ('him who bring Lickle Jesus into de New World'), and the orthography, which tries to follow the pronunciation of certain words, rather than standard English orthography (for example, 'bwai' for 'boy', 'lickle' for 'little'). However, a greater deviation from the British standard may not be a deficiency for a dialect, but may, in certain cases, be a source of strength, especially for the writing of literature. The distinctiveness of Jamaican English, for instance, has been described as giving it 'an early prominence in West Indian literature' (Chamberlin 1993: 83).

Availability, of course, is one thing. Putting the dialect into literary works is another matter. There have been critics who are against the use of dialects for the writing of literature. Norman Jeffares, for example, advocates that standard British English should be used for literatures in English outside Britain. It has also been noted that 'For a long while, the spoken language of West Indians was separated by a gulf as wide as the Atlantic from the written language of literature' (Chamberlin 1993: 80). In addition to the *theoretical* views of critics like Jeffares, it needs to be mentioned that the perennial problem of the limited readership of a work written in a dialect of English may have an effect on publishers' willingness to publish the book. For example, when James Kelman sent his first novel, *A Chancer*, to John Calder, the publisher responded by saying that 'books in Scottish dialect don't sell in England' (Jaggi 1998). However, it must be mentioned that *A Chancer* does not use Scots as extensively and insistently as *How Late It Was, How Late*.

Other languages, dialects and communication

The politics of silence

Language is used for communication. However, language may also be *avoided* in order to convey a message. In this regard, there is a great deal of truth in Stuart Hall's assertion (1991b: 51) that 'if signification depends upon the endless repositioning of its differential terms, meaning in any specific instance depends on the contingent and the arbitrary stop, the necessary break' and that 'To say anything, I have got to shut up'. Silence – in contrast to what has been said, either by oneself or others – may at times be a more powerful communicative tool than if several words were uttered.

A character who powerfully 'communicates' by remaining silent, is the tongueless Man Friday character from Coetzee's *Foe* (1986). By not being able to speak, he 'communicates' just as much, if not much more, than the original character in Defoe's novel, who subserviently speaks a pidginised version of his master's language. In Helen Tiffin's words (1989: 45), Coetzee's account 'raises the problem of white liberal complicity in his voicelessness, and the ways in which Friday has been *constructed* as voiceless by the European and continuing colonial writing of South African his/story' [Tiffin's emphasis].

With specific reference to theatre, Gilbert and Tompkins (1996: 190) have noted that 'there are at least three "silences" that are expressively deployed on the post-colonial stage: inaudibility, muteness, and refusals to speak'. Their helpful observations will be used for my discussion on the non-use of language in postcolonial theatre below.

Inaudibility, according to Gilbert and Tompkins (1996: 190), 'becomes obvious when the body's language or the proxemic signifiers are more expressive than his/her voiced utterance', as for example 'when a character cannot be heard by others on stage, but can be heard by the audience'. Muteness may be symbolic, in the sense that a character refuses to speak, and not that he cannot speak, or a character continues to suggestively but effectively 'speak', in spite of physical muteness. In the play *An Echo in the Bone*, by Dennis Scott, for example, the character called Rattler, whose tongue was cut off by his colonial master for insubordination, chooses 'to express himself through his drum rather than through the coloniser's language' (Gilbert and Tompkins 1996: 191). Another example is found in Vincent O'Sullivan's *Billy*, in which the mute Aboriginal character Billy 'speaks through' a character when he puts his hand on her shoulders. Billy later speaks on his own. However, the other characters on the stage 'assume that his "voice" is another party trick' (Gilbert and Tompkins 1996: 19). Finally, with reference to refusal to speak, there is the example of Kimathi, the Kenyan Mau Mau rebel in *The Trial of Dedan Kimathi* by Ngũgĩ wa Thiongo and Micere Githae Mugo. In the play, Kimathi 'speaks eloquently at times to his supporters' but 'is conspicuously silent during his treason trial', and is thus described as 'using silence as a tool against the colonial (in)justice system' (Gilbert and Tompkins 1996: 193).

Comprehensibility of dialects, pidgins and creoles

There is another aspect of communication that needs to be discussed here, and this has to do with problems in the use of dialects, pidgins and creoles. This is by no means a new problem. The Scottish poet Robert Burns, for example, who was believed to have written in Scots, actually did not write in authentic vernacular Scottish (McGuirk 1985: xxii). In reality, Burns's Scottish poems, in McGuirk's words (1985: xxii), 'are written in a literary language, which was mostly, although not entirely English, in grammar and syntax, and, in varying proportions, both Scottish and English in vocabulary'. Less charitably, John Lucas has described an attempt by Burns to use Scots as 'the greatest forgery of them all' (1990: 53). Had Burns truly written in Scots, he would almost certainly be a less popular poet, as fewer readers would be able to understand him.

Burns was not alone in creating an artificial language or dialect for wider comprehensibility. The twentieth-century Scottish poet Hugh MacDiarmid is more forthright in the use of a literary Scots language which is sometimes called 'synthetic Scots'. The following is an example, from his poem *The Drunk Man Looks at the Thistle*, originally published in 1926, in which the poet persona (the 'drunk man') reflects on Scotland (the 'thistle'). Interestingly, MacDiarmid (1978: 84) makes a plea for commitment to Scottish nationalists, and nationalistic causes in general, using Burns as a figure who has too often been used for the superficial expression of Scottish nationalism:

> No' wan in fifty kens a wurd Burns wrote
> But misapplied is a'body's property
> And gin there was his like alive the day
> They'd be the last a kennin 'haund to gi'e.

To MacDiarmid, the use of Scots in some of his poems is an essential part of his politics (a contrast to R.S. Thomas's poetry, where a disjunction between poetry and politics is more apparent: p. 33). Thus comprehensibility is important to him, and not mere affection for language as it is actually spoken. Otherwise, the meaning of his poems might be misunderstood, considering that Burns, whose literary Scots is not too difficult to understand by most readers of English, is not fully understood even by some Scotsmen who express superficial nationalist sentiments.

Like MacDiarmid, the Irish playwright Synge did not actually use spoken dialect. According to Cribb (1999: 108), Synge uses 'a selection from various dialects imparting a sufficient flavour to standard English for it to sound different while still remaining accessible to metropolitan audiences'. Both MacDiarmid and Synge make 'literary' languages, and do not faithfully give readers the precise dialect or variety of English actually spoken in certain parts of Scotland or Ireland. Both of them try to strike a fine balance between the nationalistic (ultimately anti-colonial) use of dialects and comprehensibility to other speakers of English.

Comprehensibility may be more seriously affected when moving out of dialects of English into pidgins, creoles or what is sometimes also known as patois, because the variation from English may be wider. In this regard, one of the reasons for the popularity, outside Nigeria, of Tutuola's first novel, *The Palm Wine Drinkard* (1952), is that it is 'a sensible compromise, between raw pidgin (which would not be intelligible to European readers) and standard English' (Dathorne 1971: 72). Creoles are generally more difficult to understand than pidgins, as they are locally based. Comprehension may be difficult not only at the international level but, occasionally, it may also be difficult for people from different regions of the same country, even if they belong to the same ethnic group. Essop Patel, who is of Indian origin, gives an example from South Africa where he notes that 'Those of us from the hinterland find it difficult to comprehend the patois of the coastal Indians which is coupled with a peculiar accent' (Wilkinson 1992: 164).

The terms pidgins and creoles are used quite frequently in discussions of further developments or extensions of world Englishes. The term patois is used less frequently and refers generally to colloquial language. Pidgins and creoles are more well-defined as terms in linguistics than patois. Pidgins and creoles arise as contact languages. A pidgin, which is believed to have originated from the mispronunciation of the word 'business', is, strictly speaking, more of a contact language than creole, as it is not anyone's native language. A pidgin comes into play primarily in the interaction between people who do not share the practical knowledge of a more established language, as in Nigeria, which has more than 250 languages and where a quarter of the population use pidgin as a contact language. A creole is more stable than a pidgin, and gains prominence when it becomes the first language or mother tongue of a group of people (for a different view, see Mufwere 2001). Accordingly, a creole usually has a richer vocabulary than a pidgin.

As a pidgin is the example *par excellence* of a language which comes into being for communicative purposes, it has the paradoxical effect of making itself, relatively speaking, more easily understood on a universal basis than a creole. Linguistically speaking, grammatical features of varieties of English-based pidgins from geographically distinct areas seem to share striking similarities. The avoidance or omission of tense markers, number concord, the copula and auxiliary verbs, for example, seem to be present in pidgins spoken in different areas of the world.

The use of pidgins in literature in English has a longer history than the use of creoles. It is claimed that pidgin was introduced into English at the beginning of the history of modern English literature by the Elizabethan dramatist Christopher Marlowe in his play *The Jew of Malta* and was also evident in the language of Man Friday in Daniel Defoe's

Robinson Crusoe (McCrum *et al.* 1986: 199). In both Marlowe's *The Jew of Malta* (published in 1633) and Defoe's *Robinson Crusoe* (1719), however, it can be argued that the pidgins used are not based on empirical observation of actual language use, but rationalizations of how they were spoken. These purported examples of pidgin are perhaps more akin to beginner's English than to actual pidgins in existence when Marlowe and Defoe wrote their works. However, there is at least one dissenting voice with regard to Defoe's use of pidgin, which will be discussed below.

As noted above, a pidgin as it appears in a creative work should not be based on a creative writer's assumption of how English is spoken by those who are not proficient in it. A pidgin's grammar usually involves some kind of simplification, as the language should be understood by people who do not have a knowledge of the grammatical intricacies of a more established language like English. However, the simplification involved may be quite different from that of beginner's English or the writer's inventive assumption of how it is spoken. As Chinua Achebe has noted – commenting on an Englishman living in Lagos who was supposed to have written a book where the pidgin 'is a sort of Uncle Tom's dialect' – Nigerian pidgin 'is a language in itself, not something you can just cook up' (Wilkinson 1992: 49).

Achebe may be referring to the language used by Joyce Cary in his novel *Mister Johnson*. However, it has been claimed that 'on a linguistic level, [Cary] has set an example for later African writers' (Boehmer 1995: 154). Boehmer's view is certainly not uncontroversial. Not only are there doubts on the accuracy of Cary's use of pidgins or other Nigerian dialects of English in the novel, but Cary's 'influence' on later African writers is perhaps more negative and more a reaction to the damage he has done, and not to be totally viewed as something positive. According to Achebe (1975: 123), while he was at the university he read 'some appalling novels about Africa (including Joyce Cary's much praised *Mister Johnson*), and decided that the story we had to tell could not be told for us by anyone else, no matter how gifted or well intentioned' (cf. Ngũgĩ 2000: 5, for a different linguistic perspective).

The faithfulness of the representation of dialects or pidgin in a creative work may indeed be used as an evaluative criterion. For example, the quality of the pidgin used in Adaora Ulasi's *Many Thing You No Understand* (1970) has been described by Oladele Taiwo (1976: 51) as 'often so poor that it constantly distracts the attention of the reader whose ears are attuned to good Pidgin'. Taiwo contrasts Ulasi's use of language to that of Achebe, whom he describes as using 'fluent standard Pidgin' in *A Man of the People*. Here is an example of pidgin in Achebe's novel (1966: 114):

> Look my frien I done tell you say if you no wan serious for this business make you go rest for house. I done see say you want play too much gentleman for this matter ... Dem tell you say na gentlemanity de give other people minister...?
>
> [ellipses in the original]

It may take a native speaker of Nigerian pidgin, such as Taiwo, to appreciate the relative closeness of the above extract to the varieties of Nigerian pidgin English.

The same criticism against Ulasi's novel can be leveled against the short story 'A Taximan's Story' and the poem '2 mothers in a h d b playground' by the Singaporean authors Catherine Lim and Arthur Yap. The use of pidgins in both works are not really faithful to pidgins actually spoken in Singapore, and this factor may have an effect on their aesthetic evaluation (Talib 1992, 1996). In this regard, turning back to a much earlier example of the use of pidgin in literature in English, N.F. Blake (1981: 113) has defended Defoe's use of pidgin in *Robinson Crusoe* by saying that it may not be totally an imaginative recreation. He proposes, against the received view on the matter, that Defoe might have been aware of some varieties of Caribbean pidgin, and thus the pidgin-like language used by Man Friday is not wholly conjectural.

As a creole may be more difficult to understand than a pidgin, a writer may choose not to write in a creole or a distinctive dialect of English, as there is the fear that he or she may not be able to communicate with people from other countries or even from other parts of a region. The writer's audience for the work will thus be reduced. Derek Walcott, for example, has a tendency to avoid creole in his plays, because it may not be understood in other areas of the Caribbean. Sam Selvon (1982: 60) adjusts the language in his novels in such a way that what we have is not full-blown creole, but a modified language which is more comprehensible to non-speakers. In this regard, Selvon (1982: 60) claims that 'I could [not] have said what I wanted to say without modifying the dialect ... the pure dialect would have been obscure and difficult to understand ... Greek to a lot of people' (also cited by Donnell and Welsh 1997: 209). Audience reception also affects text production, or constrains the possibility of publication. Roy Heath has projected that 'if you wanted to set up a publishing firm in Guyana to publish in Creolese, it isn't viable because for a start you didn't have enough people who would read it' (Jussawala and Dasenbrock 1992: 127).

With reference to the African writer, Achebe (1965: 29) has made the observation that he or she 'should aim to use English in a way that brings out his message best without altering the language to the extent that its value as a medium of international exchange will be lost'. According to Achebe (1965: 30), in a famous observation, what should emerge from the pen of the African writer is 'a new English, still in full communion with its ancestral home but altered to suit its new African surroundings'. However, there are authors, like Olive Senior in Jamaica, who write primarily for the audience in their countries and do not care too much if foreigners do not understand their stories. We have noted, in Chapter 3, the case of the Maori author Witi Ihimaera, who is not interested in communicating to English readers beyond his community. Ihimaera in fact expressed surprise when some Americans told him that they wanted to read his work: 'It is more important for it to be known in the place where it originated – where it will most have its effect – and that is in New Zealand itself' (Jussawala and Dasenbrock 1992: 225).

Lexical items

At a more restricted level, the use of isolated non-English lexical items, or those from pidgins and creoles, may also create difficulties for foreign readers, although generally to a lesser extent than their full-fledged use. Sometimes, these lexical items can be understood from their contexts within the text. If this is not the case, explanations can be given within the text itself, or the words can be translated into English later in the text, as is done by Ihimaera in his writing (see Beckman 1981: 124–8). If these strategies are inappropriate, the non-English words can be explained in a glossary at the end of the book, as in, among many other examples, the novel *The Shrimp People* (1991) by the Singaporean author Rex Shelley or the novel *Leaves of the Banyan Tree* (1979) by the Samoan writer Albert Wendt.

Sometimes, the lexical items or incidents referred to in a work are not purely linguistic, but refer to historical or social events that the foreign reader might not know, although, at the same time, disentangling them from the language spoken by the community may not always be easy. For example, Essop Patel went even further than he intended when providing a glossary for one of the poems that he was writing. He said that he 'will not only have a glossary, but explanatory notes relevant to history' and describes these as 'a new experimentation in South African poetry' (Wilkinson 1992: 171). However, these glossaries or explanations may not be able to explain the more extended use of the language, as in the more complete use of pidgins and creoles.

When an author resorts to explanations or glossaries, or avoids them, questions of communicative purpose, which are intimately connected to the work's readership, will arise. For example, the novelist Sam Selvon, who is of Trinidadian origin, uses the Trinidadian dialect of English in some of his works. However, he avoided glossaries, for he believed that the explanation, if needed, should be found in the text. However, while some indigenous words or expressions may be clear from the text, some others may be difficult to comprehend for non-Trinidadians, and these have to be sacrificed. Selvon gives the example of the Trinidadian expression 'Crapu smoke your pipe'. He has to change this to 'monkey smoke your pipe', as a non-Trinidadian might not be able to understand the word 'crapu', which refers to a toad (Jussawala and Dasenbrock 1992: 104).

Another example of the writer's strategy as regards a lexical item which may not be widely comprehended is the use, in Achebe's novel *Things Fall Apart* (1958), of the word 'harmattan', which refers to seasonal winds from the Sahara. The word is readily understood by Nigerians. Yet Achebe gives an explanation of its meaning in the text. This indicates that the novel, as Walder (1998: 11) has observed, 'was written *primarily* for an overseas audience'. Walder explains that, when it was first published, it was 'at a price few Nigerians could afford', hence the necessity of being cognizant of a non-Nigerian audience. At the same time, the fact that Achebe used the word 'harmattan' at all indicates that he also had 'a local audience in view'. But it was only later, after a cheap paperback edition was published, that the book could be read by the ordinary people in Nigeria.

Achebe's strategy here can be described in terms of what Peter Young (1971, 1973), in his discussion of West African literature in English, has called *overt cushioning*, where the explanation for the lexical item is given in the text. Another possibility is *covert cushioning*, which involves 'the fashioning of the immediate co-text into a careful context of explanation' (Young 1971: 40). Young (1973: 39) gives the following example from Elechi Amadi's *The Concubine* (1965: 35), in which the words 'okwos' and 'igele', from their textual context, clearly refer to musical instruments: 'the okwos tore the air, the drums vibrated under expert hands and the igele beat out the tempo meticulously'. Of course, there are texts where no *cushioning* is available, or the *covert cushioning* found in the text may be too subtle for many readers.

Wendt's *Leaves of the Banyan Tree*, with its glossary of Samoan words and expressions, may not be typical of literary works from the South

Pacific. Other writers from the region, such as the New Guinean Russell Soaba, leave the localised lexical items in some of their works unglossed: thus there is either *covert cushioning* or no *cushioning* at all. They do this at the expense of a wider readership. Ihimaera in fact left the Maori lexical items unglossed in one of his early works, for he intended the work to be read by fellow Maoris, only to be told by a prospective publisher that 'Maori people don't read books' (Jussawala and Dasenbrock 1992: 228). Like the case of the Jamaican Olive Senior, these writers clearly had their local audiences in mind, and were not critically concerned about the international reception of their works. However, it should be mentioned here that unglossed lexical items may not always be a barrier to a favourable international reception. Arundhati Roy for example, leaves the Malayalam words unglossed in her novel *The God of Small Things*, but this has not prevented the novel from gaining a wide international reception. Even Soaba and Ihimaera, although less famous than Roy, are certainly known outside New Guinea and New Zealand.

Importance of communication

In many ways, communication is an important consideration in postcolonial literature. Although language does play an important part, communication ultimately transcends linguistic issues to include the more holistic cultural context that a writer assumes in his work. As mentioned in Chapter 5, the use of English itself can be viewed – at least in the case of some authors – as an attempt to gain a wider audience. However, as seen earlier in this chapter, the use of dialects of English, or the introduction of some unglossed or *uncushioned* lexical items, can erect barriers to communicating with the audience or readership outside the author's country. Some critics have advised that writers should write without considering who will be reading their works, which is the advice given by Huma Ibrahim to English-language writers from the Indian subcontinent. However, Ibrahim (1998: 41) recognises at the same time that 'the question of audience remains vexed, for economic considerations will always determine a writer's modus'. Whether they 'will *always* determine a writer's modus' [my emphasis] is a moot point, but if a writer writes for a living, economic considerations do certainly play an important part.

The question of content

Language can be viewed not merely in terms of communication but also in terms of content. As Wood has noted, 'Language has always been the real theme of Indian fiction, ever since Rao Raja's *Kanthapura'* and 'There is a strong mimetic urge to capture, on the page, the music of accents and dialects' (Wood 1997: 33). Indeed, the more visible the language is in a work of literature, or the more linguistically experimental it is, the more the focus is on language itself. Visibility of language use or the experimental use of language does not draw attention away from language but makes it part of the content of the work. This can be seen in the novels of Salman Rushdie, and this is also the argument presented by Detlev Gohrbandt in relation to the Nigerian novel *The Man Who Came In From the Back of Beyond* by Biyi Bandele-Thomas. According to Gohrbandt (1996: 60), as the language in the novel 'calls attention to itself, it becomes one of the themes in the novel'. Bandele-Thomas's use of language in his novel does not always call attention to itself clearly on the surface, in the way that Rushdie's language in his novels does. Here is an exception from the novel, in which a person who is reluctant to give away information is questioned by a detective (Bandele-Thomas 1991: 125):

> 'Your name, smarty, or don't you know your name?'
> 'Is it my name or my father's name you want?'
> Detective Sergeant Mubi was legendary for his exceptionally cool temper. 'Your name, smarty,' he said.
> 'You see,' Daniel explained, 'my old man was called Stephen Daniel Steven.'
> 'And you?'
> 'They call me Steven Daniel Stephen,' Daniel explained.
> 'And where is the difference?' Mubi asked in exasperation.
> 'Well, they called the old man Danny. Danny Sparkle, they used to say. But me they call Daniel. Daniel in the lion's den.'
> 'Welcome, Dan, to the lion's den.'

Names and the things they are supposed to represent is one of the thematic threads centring on language running through the novel.

Politics of using other languages and dialects

The reason why a writer chooses to use a particular dialect or variety of English may not be merely a superficial or 'innocent' stylistic consideration, but there may be political reasons for doing so. The word politics here is used both more widely, from one angle, and, more specifically, from another, in the sense that it is wider than its usual denotation, and it more specifically refers to linguistic politics. In this connection, linguistic politics has always been an important concern, especially among writers from the other nations of Britain. For example, it has been noted that 'a variety of Scottish writers, from Galt to Stevenson and Douglas Brown, deployed and redeployed Scots throughout the nineteenth century as a means of both questioning and supplementing the dominant monodialectal diction of "standard English" ' (Crawford 1992: 174). There are, of course, other political reasons for using dialects, pidgins and creoles.

Linguistic politics is of course also a concern for writers outside the British Isles. For example, in Segun Oyebunde's play *Katakata for Sofahead*, which is set in a prison, the use of a Nigerian variety of pidgin English is described by Gilbert and Tompkins (1996: 187) as a means to establish 'in language a site for anti-colonial activity in Nigeria'. Gilbert and Tompkins (1996: 188) go on to describe the use of pidgin in the play as investing the prisoners 'with a power that their incarceration denies them: the ability to enforce their own linguistic freedom'.

Other examples of writers who choose to use a particular dialect or variety of English for political reasons are three women originally from the Caribbean: Jamaica Kincaid, Marlene Nourbese Philip and Michelle Cliff. Kincaid's attitude towards the use of standard British English finds expression in her view that standard English is 'the language of the criminal who committed the crime' (cited by Skinner 1998: 19). According to Philip, who describes English as a 'foreign l/anguish' (cited by Boehmer 1995: 207), 'the havoc that was wreaked upon the English language' in their works 'metaphorically expresses the experience of the African being brought to the New World and all the havoc that that entailed for them' (Philip 1990: 275).

Thus standard English has a hegemonic influence and prevents the language as it is spoken by the common people from being used. According to Cliff, one 'needs to unlearn the very hegemony of the King's English in order to approximate an "authentic" vision of a precolonial, uncolonized, prior self' (Aegerter 1997: 901). She is of the view that if the language of the common people is negated in the colonial equation then the culture that is associated with the language will be erased. With reference to the Jamaican situation, there is thus the fear that the language as it is found on the island may be creatively erased from her works: that 'the "first language" of Jamaicans is not granted validity' (Aegerter 1997: 902). As a result, she 'mixes patois with standard English to disrupt and to "stretch" English to her resistant purposes' (Aegerter 1997: 902). Indeed, according to Cliff, the use of patois may represent a rebellion against what she describes as 'fluent' English: the English that she was familiar with during her stay in

England. In her words, 'against a history of forced fluency was the beginning of a journey into speech' (Cliff 1985: 12).

The use of dialect or pidgin may not necessarily extend throughout the work to serve its political purpose. There are some works where dialect or pidgin is used only partially, but the political purpose is equally well served. In the play *Capricornia*, by the Australian writer Louis Nowra, the story of David and Goliath is 'translated' into what has been described as 'an oral performance in Pidgin' by the half-Aboriginal character Tody, who turns it into 'a full-blown carnivalesque parody' (Gilbert and Tompkins 1996: 45). As a result, she annoys her teacher. The parody of the story of David and Goliath subverts the Christian myth, thus making a political statement to the character about its inadequacy when it is expressed in standard English.

Linguistic politics should not only be viewed in terms of the use of dialects, pidgins or creoles. Style is also important. The link between style and politics, for example, is clearly put by the Scottish writer James Kelman, with reference to his own works:

> I didn't want to work within someone else's value system that inferiorised my people – which is what English literature is. So I had to make use of their language and transform it into something that could be mine. Part of that process is to purify the language into a value-free prose, where everything's concrete; no abstract nouns, adjectives, adverbs. [quoted in Jaggi 1998)

Thus, it is not only the use of Scottish dialect that is of political significance in Kelman's work, but the style in which the dialect is used.

The question of acceptability

Some readers may have a positive attitude towards certain non-standard English dialects, or to some English-based pidgins and creoles. In general, the positive attitude is growing. At the international level, Ngũgĩ's decision to write his creative works in Gĩkũyũ, although it also meant a rejection of English, has been influential in encouraging authors to write in pidgins, creoles or other dialects of English. The Guyanan Roy Heath, for example, has been encouraged by Ngũgĩ's example to write his creative works in creole, or what is called *nation language* in the Caribbean (see Chapters 4 and 5). It must be mentioned, however, that, in spite of his influence, Ngũgĩ's attitude towards pidgin English has not been entirely complimentary. This is his reply to the question of whether pidgin could be 'a relevant medium of communication':

For everyone who speaks pidgin, there are thousands who speak their own languages, and even those who speak pidgin English or other sorts of English nevertheless have their own fully fledged national language to which they have access.

(Jussawala and Dasenbrock 1992: 30)

In other words, Ngũgĩ fears that use of pidgin English by writers would result in the neglect of their own native languages.

There is, occasionally, an erstwhile positive attitude towards a variety of English at the national level. In Belize, for example, as noted in Zee Edgell's novel *Beka Lamb* (1982: 11–12), the variety of creole spoken by the general population is 'regarded as a language to be proud of by most people in the country' and 'served as a means of communication amongst the races'. Accordingly, Edgell's novel does not fight shy of using Belizean creole in the dialogue.

However, the positive attitude towards dialects, pidgins and creoles is not universal. On the one hand is the complete turning away from English, as seen above in the example of Ngũgĩ, who believes that the author should use his or her own native language instead of resorting to pidgin. On the other is the turning inwards towards a more standard variety of English, with the accompanying belief that varieties which differ significantly from standard English should be avoided. For instance, in Jean Rhys's *The Wide Sargasso Sea* (1968), one of the reasons for the (unnamed) Rochester's growing dislike of his wife, Antoinette Cosway, is her use of the Jamaican variety of English.

The negative attitude towards dialects, pidgins and creoles is not only found within the fictional world. Even more important is what goes on outside the fictional world. In fact, attitudes towards language in fiction are very often reflective of, or are affected by, what goes on outside it. Specifically, the author or, more frequently perhaps, the readers may not regard the use of certain varieties of English as 'acceptable'. This attitude may be due to prejudice, of which Rochester's attitude, in Rhys's novel, towards the English used by his wife is a reflection. Linguistic attitudes thus have a social dimension, but they also have an aesthetic dimension, although, admittedly, it is not always easy to separate the social from the aesthetic in this regard. The readers' view may have an effect on the author's practice: if readers do not find the dialect or language acceptable, the author has to accommodate their view, prejudiced as it may be, by not using it, even if he or she is more sympathetic towards it.

The prejudice against non-mainstream varieties of English is not new. It has always existed in the history of literature in English. There is, according to Robert Crawford (1992: 57–8), the insistent avoidance of dialectal representation of speech by the Scottish writer Tobias Smollett, for the main character in the novel *Roderick Random* (1748):

> ... in a novel linguistically alert to speech mannerisms and to French, Welsh, and Irish accents among the minor characters, Roderick's Scottishness of speech is never represented on the page. The result is that the reader, though kept aware that the protagonist is a Scot, tends to sense his voice as standard English. This is surely a deliberate ploy on the part of Smollett to win over non-Scottish-speaking readers to Roderick's side...

This, however, does not mean that Roderick invariably uses standard English in his speech in the fictional world. Crawford (1992: 58) notices that 'Other characters in the book hear Roderick's Scottish accent. We are made aware of it, but do not hear it directly' (see also Blake 1981: 113–4).

The negative attitude towards non-standard varieties is perhaps more evident towards dialects or varieties found further away from England. For example, Lal and Rao (1959: vi), who are editors of a volume of Indian poetry in English, display a hierarchy of acceptability with regard to the different varieties or dialects of English: 'King's and Queen's English, yes; Indian English, permissible; pidgin, bombastic and gluey English, no'.

Some people may find certain dialects of English 'funny', in both the sense that they are humorous and the sense that they are peculiar. Burns, for example, did not write in authentic vernacular Scottish but he has also been accused of finding Scots English 'funny', and has a condescending attitude towards it, which is especially evident in some of his humorous poems (Traugott and Pratt 1980: 337–8). Rightly or wrongly, sympathy for characters in literary works who use dialects may be lost in readers' eyes, and writers are very often aware of this. Smollett, for example, tries to manipulate the readers' sympathy for Roderick Random by making his Scottish accent less evident on the surface of the novel. However, for some authors, the 'funny' nature of English dialects may also depend on the way the dialects, or the characters using them, are presented in the literary work, and not necessarily by the use of the dialects *per se*.

This is the case with Nissim Ezekiel's poem 'Goodbye Party for Miss Pushpa T.S.' A reading of the poem is quite often greeted with laughter, not because of its use of a variety of Indian English but because of the way it is used, which has irritated some of Ezekiel's readers and listeners. Here are some lines from the poem (in Parthasarathy 1976: 37):

> You are all knowing, friends,
> what sweetness is in Miss Pushpa.
> I don't mean only external sweetness
> but internal sweetness.
> Miss Pushpa is smilling and smiling
> even for no reason
> but simply because she is feeling.

A distinct feature found in some varieties of Indian English is the frequent appearance of the '-ing' construction where it is normally avoided in standard or other varieties of English. Ezekiel deploys this feature to humorous effect in the above lines.

After Ezekiel's reading of 'Miss Pushpa' at the Indian Embassy in London, someone asked him, 'Aren't you being insulting to Indian people who speak like this?' (Walder 1998: 91). Ezekiel mentioned that the question was asked whenever he read the poem in India. His attitude towards Indian English can thus be regarded as ambivalent. In this regard, Gauri Deshpande (n.d.: 13) has noted that although Ezekiel is the exception in making 'a serious effort to change the standard English learnt from textbooks', he 'spoils the effort, finally, by writing "down", or with a humorous intent only, in Indian English'.

However, before closing the discussion on the attitude towards the acceptability of non-standard dialects of English, and English-based pidgins and creoles, it should be mentioned again that this attitude has become more positive over the years. In the case of South Africa, for example, it has been noted that 'Up to the 1960s, the respect accorded to standard British English as a literary model ensured that the literature produced by South Africans rarely betrayed its local linguistic underpinnings' (Fitzmaurice 1999: 166). From the 1960s onwards, however, the use of local linguistic features found in South Africa has become more common.

Orthography

Orthography may play a part in representing other dialects of English, or of pidgins and creoles. With reference to the representation of dialects of English in British literature, N.F. Blake (1981: 15) has noted that it is the 'most important aspect of non-standard language in literature' when compared with vocabulary and syntax. One of the reasons for its importance is the increasing stability of spelling in the early history of Modern English, which allows dialects to become more easily represented – at least as far as their pronunciation is concerned – by deviating from the standard spelling.

However, the use of different spelling from standard English orthography in literature is not totally uncontroversial. Sam Selvon, for example, gives an explanation of why he avoids it:

> I didn't use d-e for t-h-e; I feel t-h-e is fine with me. When I open a book, I look at a sentence, I look at the writing of it, and I say that's ok if the rhythm of the dialect is still there. I feel that writing in phonetics jars the reader. I've heard many people say that reading different dialects with phonetic spelling is a bit irritating, having to analyze it all in your mind.
>
> (Jussawala and Dasenbrock 1992: 105)

In the following sentence from *The Lonely Londoners* (1956), the use of a variety of Caribbean English is unmistakable, but Selvon does not alter the spelling, even retaining the 'th' spelling in 'the' and 'that', even though it is likely that it would be pronounced as 'd': 'Come a time when the warden of the hostel tired hearing Cap talk about the allowance that coming and never come, and tell him he have to leave' (Selvon 1972: 33).

8 How's the mixture?

English, dialects and other languages

Describing vs. demonstrating dialect and language

There are two broad ways that dialects or languages can be represented in a work of literature: either by describing the dialect or language used, or by actually using it. In the analysis of fiction, the language of the narrator in third-person narratives should also be distinguished from that of the characters. This distinction may not be valid in first-person narration, as the first-person narrator is virtually a character in the fictional world; the language of the first-person narrator can therefore be treated together with that of the characters.

It is in the language of the third-person narrator that examples of the description of language use, instead of its demonstration, generally occur. The actual use of another language may involve *code-mixing* or *-switching*, which will be explained below. Describing the language being used instead of actually using it may result in the avoidance of code-mixing or switching altogether, at least on the surface of the work. This does seem to be the simpler alternative, as the writer need not write the other language down and need not worry about the audience's comprehension of what is written in the language. This is seen, among many other examples, in the following sentence from Timothy Mo's *Sour Sweet* (1983: 135), which gives a stylistic contrast of a character's use of English and Cantonese through the indirect means of description: 'Her voice, so expressive and live in her native Cantonese, became shrill, peremptory and strangely lifeless in its level pitching when she spoke in English.' Here is another example from *Echoes of Silence* by the Malaysian novelist Chuah Guat Eng:

> They had spoken in a mixture of Chinese and English, which I found by turns funny and incomprehensible, but they had communicated. Here my mother and I spoke in textbook English, almost untainted

by Malaysianisms, because that was the way she had always spoken and had taught me to speak.

(Chuah 1994: 217)

Representing 'standard' and 'non-standard' in fictional technique

As the language of the third-person narrator is not directly related to any of the characters' use of language, it is usually quite close to what is regarded as the standard in a particular socio-cultural or national context. The language of the characters or of the first-person narrator, being of a more personal nature, is usually at more liberty from the standard or from formal usage, and is thus ideal for the demonstration of language use instead of its mere description. As such, it allows greater facility in the use of varieties of English which differ from the standard, such as in Jean Rhys's short story 'Let Them Call It Jazz' (1962), in which the first-person narrator, who is a white Dominican, uses a dialect of English to depict the voice of a black person exiled from the country. However, generally speaking, the first-person narrator may be relatively less liberal in his or her language use, as the non-fictional audience to whom the narrative is addressed has to be taken into account, which one suspects is also the case with Rhys's story. According to Kenneth Ramchand (1988: 105), Rhys, with her audience in mind, actually presents a modified dialect in her story and urges the reader to imagine 'the voice of a dialect-speaking character even when the language looks like Standard English'. One can disagree with Ramchand, as the extract below (Rhys 1968: 164) certainly does not look like it is in standard English:

> This man is not at all like most English people. He see very quick, and he decide very quick. English people take long time to decide – you three quarter dead before they make up their mind about you. Too besides, he speak very matter of fact, as if it's nothing. He speak as if he realize well what it is to live like I do – that's why I accept and go.

The lack of number concord – 'He see … he decide…' – and the use of the present tense where the past tense ought to be used are not features of standard English, even Caribbean standard English (see Trudgill and Hannah 1994: Chapter 6). It is interesting to compare the above with the use of creole (see pp. 136 and 139) in Sam Selvon's *Lonely Londoners*. The white man through which the character speaks has a distancing effect in Rhys's story, as it shelters the narrative from being a faithful reflector of the dialect. It also acts as a channel through which a language that is comprehensible to most of her readers can be filtered.

Although less common, deviations from the standard or formal usage in the language of the third-person narrator can also be found. In complex examples of speech presentation in third-person narratives, the distinction between the language of the third-person narrator and that of the characters may not be clear-cut. Because of this lack of a clear-cut distinction, deviations from the standard or formal usage can be found in the language used by the third-person narrator. However, such deviations can also be seen in simpler narratives, in which case the notion of the language *standard* being used in the work has to be redefined. In other words, some of the deviations may be indicators of how the standard language of the community differs from standard British English.

However, sometimes the deviations are more extensive, so that what is generally used in the work is not the standard English found in the particular community but a dialect, creole or pidgin. These examples of language use apply different norms to those assumed by the community – usually implicitly – with regard to what its standard English should be. When the third-person narrator uses language which differs significantly from the standard, we are dealing, as pointed out by Christian Mair (1996: 239), with vernacular or with dialect literature.

In Caribbean literature, two prominent examples of the third-person narrator's more extensive use of creole than is normally expected are Victor S. Reid's *New Day* (1949) and Sam Selvon's *The Lonely Londoners*. An example from Selvon's novel has been quoted earlier (p. 136). Here is another example: 'It have people living in London who don't know what happening in the room next to them, far more the street, or how other people living' (Selvon 1972: 58). Proficiency in the creole used by Selvon is not needed in order to understand the sentence: 'There are people in London who don't know what's happening in the next room, let alone in the street, or how people are living elsewhere'. Two striking grammatical features are the use of 'It' and the verb 'to have' instead of 'There' followed by the verb 'to be' for existential clauses; and the deletion of the auxiliary verb in the progressive '-ing' constructions, as in 'what happening' instead of 'what is happening'.

Selvon's novel does appear to be particularly successful in its language use. Other Caribbean writers, such as Wilson Harris and Roy Heath, have expressed their admiration of Selvon's language in his work. Wilson Harris specifically commends Selvon for making 'dialect part of the consciousness of the narrator' (Jussawala and Dasenbrock 1992: 105).

Another work which can be seen as belonging to this category is Lorna

Goodison's short story 'Bella Makes Life' (see the analysis in Mair 1996). Stretches of Goodison's story can be taken as examples of the complex presentation of speech noted above, in which the distinction between the language of the third-person narrator and that of the characters may not be clear-cut. However, some of the examples of creole usage in the story cannot be attributed to the speech or thought of any of the characters, and they have to be included as part of the linguistic norms of the third-person narrator, and, consequently, the language generally used in the work should be redefined.

Reasons for the use of pidgins, creoles and other dialects of English

There are several reasons for the use of other dialects of English, or of fully fledged pidgins or creoles. Some of the political reasons have been discussed above. Another reason is the attempt to infuse a sense of realism into the work, as in Cyprian Ekwensi's *Jagua Nana*, in which, according to Izevbaye (1974: 142), 'The social realism of the novel is enriched by the almost literally transcribed pidgin speech of the characters'. Izevbaye further notes that 'pidgin belongs to urban Nigeria'. It is thus not merely realism *per se* which is achieved by the use of a variety of Nigerian pidgin in Ekwensi's novel, but geographical realism, in the sense that the language used in his novel represents urban speech, which can also be found, more successfully perhaps, in Achebe's novels (Chukwukere 1969: 21). A further use of pidgin is to indicate a character's lack of education, as in Saro-Wiwa's *The Wheel: A Farce in Six Situations*, in which a lower level of literacy is indicated through the use of a variety of Nigerian pidgin. The following is an extract from the *Sixth Situation* (Saro-Wiwa 1989: 76):

> CHIEF MINISTER: I want to see the Chairman of the Corporation.
> SECURITY GUARD: Why for?
> CHIEF MINISTER: It's private.
> SECURITY GUARD: Private, ehn?
> CHIEF MINISTER: Yes.
> SECURITY GUARD: Wettin be dis place? Not office? Dis na office. If you wan see Sheerman for private you must to go to his house. Dis na office time.
> CHIEF MINISTER: But what I have to tell him is official.
> SECURITY GUARD: You wan see de Sherman for private to talk to am official. Which kain foolish be dat. If na private, na private, if na official, na official. Which one dey?

CHIEF MINISTER: I am a busy man. I have no time for this rigmarole.

Another reason for the use of pidgin, according to Chinua Achebe, is its brevity, in some contexts, when compared with the use of more standard Englishes. For example, the following sentence in pidgin from Achebe's *Anthills of the Savanna* (1987) would look long-drawn-out and clumsy if rendered in standard English, 'You think na so we do am come reach superintendent'. The contrast can be clearly sensed in Achebe's translation of the sentence in standard English: 'Do you think this is how I have worked all these years and succeeded in becoming Superintendent?' (Jussawala and Dasenbrock 1992: 74). In addition to lack of brevity, the sentence in standard English would also look too formal, and thus less realistic, given the situation.

Sometimes, the appearance of a dialect of English in a literary work may be tied to the genre of the work, or to some features of the literature from the region that the work comes from. For example, Ramchand has noted that 'West Indian literature would seem to be the only substantial literature in which the dialect-speaking character is the central character' (1974: 194). Of course, dialect-speaking main characters are not rare, but it is really the persistence of this pattern which makes it noticeable in West Indian literature in English. The reason for the use of a different dialect of English, or of a pidgin or creole, may date back even further, as it has been claimed that it is the bearer (with reference to the use of creole in Caribbean poetry of the sixties and seventies) 'of lexical and idiomatic reference to elements of African culture' (Rodríguez 1996: 29).

Using dialects, languages and switching them

As in the case of the novels *New Day* by Reid and *The Lonely Londoners* by Selvon, and the play *Katakata for Sofahead* by Oyebunde, all of which have been mentioned earlier, a complete work may be in a pidgin, creole or dialect of English. Some of the poems of David Dabydeen and Grace Nichols, for example, are written entirely in Guyanese creole. Another example of a work written entirely in creole or pidgin is Ken Saro-Wiwa's *Soza Boy* (1985), which uses Nigerian pidgin. Here is an extract from Saro-Wiwa's novel (1985: 84):

> I am telling you, many things were crossing my mind as we were digging those pits. We were digging when the sun commot. We were digging when the sun was shining proper and you cannot see shadow.

We were digging when the sun begin to die and our shadow come long. We were still digging when the sun don die finish and porson no fit see him brother again. And you know, all this time that we are digging, we no chop anything. Even to see water to drink we no see at all.

The above passage is not too difficult to understand. The lexical items 'commot' and 'porson' clearly refer to 'come out' and 'person', and are spelt in such a way in order to imitate the pronunciation in the variety of Nigerian pidgin which the novel attempts to represent. Other features distinctive to the variety are the use of the word 'proper' to mean 'brightly'; the use of the word 'chop' to mean 'eat'; and the non-use of determiners before singular nouns, or the avoidance of plural morphemes for plural nouns: 'you cannot see shadow', and, more specifically with regard to the latter, 'our shadow come long'

But quite often, only parts of a work use a dialect, pidgin or creole. Before turning to code-mixing or -switching, which is a rather frequently encountered process by which a person changes from one language or dialect to another, one interesting possibility in the use of one or more languages or dialects must be mentioned: the use of an entire language side by side with English. This can be seen in novels and poetry. Two celebrated instances of the this are T.S. Eliot's *The Wasteland* and Ezra Pound's *The Cantos*. However, the sustained use of another language or dialect together with English or a standard variety of English is more commonly found in drama. In contrast to Eliot's and Pound's works, dramatic works usually make use of ordinary language rather than quotations from high literature. In the play *Balconville*, by the Canadian playwright David Fennario, both French and English have equal footing, and in the play *The Blinkards*, by the Ghanaian playwright Kabina Sekyi, both English and Akan are used. In Ngũgĩ's unpublished play *Maitũ Njugĩra* (*Mother Sing For Me*), three languages are used to represent the languages of three different classes. Even more languages and dialects are used in *Mama Looking for Her Cat*, by the Singaporean playwright Kuo Pao Kun. Not surprisingly, one of the main themes of Kuo's work is miscommunication between people who speak difference languages or dialects.

In code-mixing or switching, dialects or creoles are not only presented side by side, but occasional linguistic shifts can be seen in the language use of particular characters. Code-mixing involves the use of a scattering of words in a different language or dialect, whereas code-switching involves something more substantial: a whole clause or a sizeable phrase from the other language or dialect is imported (for discussions of code-switching in postcolonial literary works see Omole 1998 and Gordon and Williams 1998). Some linguists, however, do not make a distinction between the two, whereas others prefer the term code-switching over code-mixing, as it is difficult to distinguish the latter from *borrowing*, which will be discussed below.

Is it really code-switching? Borrowing and interference

Code-switching should be distinguished from borrowing. As pointed out by Braj Kachru (1986: 9, 65–6), code-switching 'is not borrowing in the sense of filling a lexical gap'. It involves the incorporation of aspects of the grammar of the other language as well. The incorporation of *lexical items* from another language may hinge on *lexical borrowings* from the other language, and not code-switching. In lexical borrowing, the difficulty may be restricted to the non-English lexical items and not the incorporation of the grammar of the non-English language. Thus glossaries may be helpful for lexical borrowings but less useful or relevant for code-switching.

Another feature involving two languages is *interference*. This occurs when one language shows an influence on another, or intrudes on its grammar. Broadly speaking, code-switching can be regarded as a case of interference, but of a relatively more predictable kind. In code-switching, the knowledge of the languages and dialects involved is shared more broadly by the members of a particular community of speakers, whereas this is not necessarily the case with interference. Interference may be a factor in learning the English language: patterns are brought over from another language even if one is proficient in English.

An explanation of interference at work can be found in the following description by the Chicana author Sandra Cisneros of the intrusion of Spanish in the English used in her novel *The House on Mango Street* (1983):

> If you take *Mango Street* and translate it, it's Spanish. The syntax, the sensibility, the diminutives, the way of looking at inanimate objects – that's not a child's voice as is sometimes said. That's Spanish! I didn't notice that when I was writing.
>
> (Jussawala and Dasenbrock 1992: 288)

One reason why Cisneros was not aware that she was practically writing Spanish with English words, is that her base language, Spanish, had *interfered* with her use of English (1989: 33):

You can never have too much sky. You can fall asleep and wake up drunk on sky, and sky can keep you safe when you are sad. Here there is too much sadness and not enough sky. Butterflies too are few and so are flowers and most things that are beautiful.

There is a poetic, almost surreal quality to Cisneros's prose, but she herself does not deny that this may be partly due to the unconscious interference of Spanish as the base language. If she had more specifically employed code-switching, she would probably be more conscious of switching between English and Spanish, but this is not the case above.

However, the writer may also consciously introduce elements of interference in a literary work. These elements cannot be easily described as examples of code-switching, as their presence in the work cannot be explained in terms of actual language use outside the fictional world. Neither can they be appropriately described as borrowings, for they are not examples of foreign loanwords introduced into the text because of the lack of the appropriate lexical items in the English language. Examples of conscious interference can be found in G.V. Desani's novel *All About H. Hatterr* (1948). In Desani's novel, there is, according to Braj Kachru (1995: 4), the intrusion of 'Sanskrit compounding *(samasa)* ... such as "Ruler of the firmament; Son of the mighty-bird, ..." "Thy sister my darling, thy name?" ' Thus English words are used, but there is a clear cultural intervention from a foreign language, Sanskrit in this instance.

Knowledge of other languages

Although the main interest here is in English-language literature, there are a number of non-English literary texts which use English as a secondary language for code-switching. An example is the Spanish version of Rolando Hinojosa's *Dear Rafe* (1985), in which code-mixing with English as the second language has an important contribution to make to the interpretation of the work. Hinojosa's *Dear Rafe* – or rather the title for its Spanish version, *Mi querido Rafa* (1981) – is a clear example of a work whose use of another language may be too demanding for the reader.

There are other works in which the required knowledge of another language may not be so obvious. For example, the work may give almost equal weight to two or more languages, or more weight to the non-English language or languages, to the extent that the reader needs to be proficient in them in order to understand the work. The use of languages side by side, such as in the plays *Balconville* by Fennario, *Maitū*

Njugīra by Ngũgĩ and *Mama Looking for Her Cat* by Kuo, have been mentioned above. It is clearly difficult to use glossaries for such works, especially when they are performed, because of the sustained or extended usage of other languages. In order to make readers or members of the audience who do not understand the languages understand the passages as they are read or performed, they may have to be completely translated. This is of course self-defeating, and there are tremendous disadvantages in doing so. The writer, therefore, may not be in favour of translation being in the same volume as the printed text or as a printed appendage to the performed play.

Even more complicated than the use of languages side by side is the code-mixing of two or more languages where the non-English languages are given such prominence that proficiency in them is needed in order to understand the work. Translations are virtually impossible here. In addition to Hinojosa's *Mi querido Rafa*, mentioned previously, he cites some of the early works of his fellow Chicano writer Alurista, saying 'you have to be absolutely bilingual to read them' (Jussawala and Dasenbrock 1992: 263). The following observation by the Malaysian writer Lloyd Fernando is also a clear instance where the use of more than one language may create difficulties, although it is not clear if this was a case of using two languages side by side or, as Fernando (1997: 8) prefers to describe it, of code-mixing:

> Another fairly recent play, KL-KO by Ann Lee, took code-switching to the maximum extent possible. Act 1 Scene 3 has a pervasive stage direction for the entire scene which says, "Following dialogue should be in Hokkien (Penang accent) with Malaysian English at times." Act 1 Scene 4 has a similar stage direction: "Following dialogue should be mostly in Bahasa Malaysia (Penang accent) but with Malaysian English at times." Finally, to cap it all off, Act 2 Scene 17 specifies a certain character who "may translate in BM [Bahasa Malaysia], Mandarin, Hindi/Tamil, French, German as well as English". ... The danger of the method is that you can be just frivolous, or laugh at the characters rather than with them.

Judging code-mixing or switching

Clearly, opinion can be divided on whether to resort to code-switching or to avoid it altogether. The use of code-switching in a literary work may depend on the author's need to reflect the accuracy of language use by the characters. A speaker may switch to another language or back to English 'in response to the nature of the situation, to the participants, the purpose of the interaction, the topic of conversation or something else that is relevant to the context' (Fitzmaurice 1999: 167). In Hinojosa's *Mi querido Rafa*, the main character, Rafe (or Rafa in the original), begins, according to the author, 'with a lot of Spanish, but as the bank job becomes more and more with him, the Spanish begins to be invaded by English' (Jussawala and Dasenbrock 1992: 260). Thus English appears to be a more prestigious or more formal language in the context of Hinojosa's novel, as it has an association with one's profession, whereas Spanish is the language of home. Avoidance of this switch between the two languages, or other switches, given the appropriate contexts, may make the work appear unnatural.

The accuracy or appropriateness of these switches is usually dependent on native speaker judgments. With reference to Hinojosa's novel, the native speaker is a bilingual Chicano speaker who has Spanish as his mother tongue and English as a second language. It is this native speaker who may be the best judge of whether and where the switches should be found, and how they work out from a processual perspective.

The use of code-switching may be judged not only in terms of the accuracy of linguistic representation, but also on aesthetic grounds. For example, whether too much or too little code-switching is used in a work in a certain context is partly an aesthetic question, and not merely a reflection of the faithfulness of language use. The following is a qualified negative judgement by an Indian scholar on the use of code-mixing in Indian works in English; it is also an expression of the familiar question of whether English should be used at all in Indian works of literature:

> After the original sin of writing in English, it is suggested, atonement can be made by concocting an English that is Indian. The word 'concocting' is used since some authors seek to write Indian English simply by importing into English an adequate number of italicised Indian words.
>
> (Rajan 1974: 84)

What Rajan refers to here may not be code-mixing or -switching, which were highlighted above, but borrowing.

However, judgements on code-mixing are not only based on aesthetic grounds and on the accuracy of linguistic representation, for there are cultural and political dimensions to them as well. The various ways by which phrases from another language are used in a literary text have been described, for example, in terms of 'literary strategies which subtly express cultural conflicts through linguistic tensions' (Karrer and Lutz

1990: 25). In this context, to return to Rajan's view, writing Indian English is not simply a matter of conveniently importing into English a sufficient number of italicised Indian words, but there are serious cultural and ultimately political considerations at work when the writer resorts to code-mixing. In this regard, Kachru (1986: 9), has pointed out that English is sometimes used in code-mixing 'to *neutralize* identities one is reluctant to express by the use of native languages or dialects'.

Other stylistic considerations apart from code-mixing

Speech presentation

The distinction between the language of the narrator and that of the characters noted above is essentially part of *speech presentation* in fiction. In this connection, the presentation of the language of the third-person narrator is usually quite close to what is regarded as the standard, in whatever way that 'standard' is defined (Trudgill and Hannah 1994; Bauer 1994; Bex and Watts 1999). The presentation of the language of the characters, however, has more variation from the standard. In addition to their own idiosyncrasies of speech, the characters have social affiliations that make their speech quite distinctive. A similar distinction is observed by Dennis Walder (1998: 44) in the disjunction between the 'narrative voice' in the fiction and non-fiction of Naipaul, which to him is 'always standard English', and the language of his characters, who 'speak in local varieties'. However, instead of seeing this as a natural tendency in fictional writing, and having a general application, Walder attributes the source of this disjunction to Naipaul's belief, quoted in Chapter 5 of this book, that the English language 'was mine' whereas 'the tradition was not'. It is difficult to agree with Walder's observation, as the disjunction between the 'standard English' of the 'narrative voice', and the local varieties spoken by the characters, can be found not only in Naipaul's works but in numerous other works.

Oral influence of non-English languages

The influence of the writer's native spoken language may be strong, even if he or she does not speak it, or no longer speaks it as fluently as English. The influence of oral literature on the works of African authors has been mentioned in Chapters 4 and 6, and of Irish Gaelic on Anglo-Irish authors in Chapter 4. The American-based Indian-born writer Meena Alexander has noted that although it is true that 'I don't read or write Malayalam', the language 'is a very powerful oral presence to me' and 'people have sometimes felt that maybe the rhythm of my writing is drawn from Malayalam' (Mohanty 1997). Sometimes, the effect of the writer's native spoken language on written English may be more consciously achieved, as in the case of the Samoan novelist Albert Wendt. Jacqueline Bardolph (1984: 51) has noted that:

> In [Wendt's] best works one can hear echoes of the oral rhythm of traditional texts, and of the spoken voice generally. He is not just transcribing patterns of speech, but achieves an effective stylisation of oral characteristics for the written medium.

Apart from spoken language as a whole, oral literature, more specifically, oral poetry, may have an influence on written literature. The extent of the influence may depend on the subject matter and genre of the written work. According to Donatus Nwoga (1990: 102), 'the formal influence of oral poetry on the written tradition of Africa is greatest in those poems which deal with uncomplicated emotions and issues such as lament, anger, protest', as seen, for example, in Christopher Okigbo's *Path of Thunder*, Okot p'Bitek's *Songs*, Kofi Awoonor's *Songs of Sorrow*, and Oswald Mtshali's and Dennis Brutus's protest poems.

Mass communication

Apart from speech in face-to-face interaction, other distinctive styles representing other modes of communication need to be depicted. Among the most important is speech associated with the radio, the press and television. Examples of speech in these media can be described as essentially monologic, unlike the dialogic nature of face-to-face conversational interaction, as the audience is not present to interact with the speakers. They are subject to local linguistic influences, although usually less distinctively than in informal conversational interaction. Among the authors who have represented these modes of communication is V.S. Naipaul, as seen in the radio broadcasts in his *In a Free State* (1971) and *Guerillas* (1975) (see discussion in Zapata 1996).

Using English as if it is another language

There are occasions when a multilingual or multidialectal situation has to be portrayed, but the use of code-switching may be inappropriate to the situation. Using two languages side by side may also not be appropriate, as the writer may be committed to write in English, and uses it even if another language is supposed to be spoken. The Indian novelist Mulk Raj Anand, for example, claims that much of the English dialogue of his novel *Untouchable* should actually be in Punjabi or Hindustani. Here is an example of speech from *Untouchable* (1940: 80):

> Babu ji, Babu ji, God will make you prosperous. Please make my message reach the ears of the Hakim ji. I have been shouting, shouting, and have even asked some people to tell the Hakim Sahib that I have a prayer to make to him.

As Anand's novel is written in English, the dialogues have to be in English. However, the idiomatic expressions in the original language will be lost if they are rendered in English. The above is a successful attempt to ensure that at least some of the flavour of the original language is not lost when a speech is rendered in English.

It has been claimed by the readers of Raja Rao's novel *Kanthapura* (1938) that it is practically a representation in English of Rao's native language, Kannada. According to Dasenbrock, 'Much of *Kanthapura* reads as if it were translated from Kannada; the syntactic patterns are those of Kannada, though the work is in English' (Jussawala and Dasenbrock 1992: 154). There are even some examples of literary works in which the authors try not only to imitate another language but, more specifically, the linguistic patterns used in a literary work written in the language. For example, Aurobindo Ghose tries to 'catch something of the Upanishadic movement so far as it is possible in English' in his lengthy poem *Savitri* (1950), although his effort has not met with aesthetic success (Parthasarathy 1976: 2). A sustained attempt by the Nigerian author Gabriel Okara to comprehensively use English as if it is another language will be discussed in more detail below.

The author's translation or conversion of a local language into English in a literary work may come at a heavy price. Emecheta, for example, declares that English 'is not my emotional language', and when she tries to render a passage in Igbo into English 'it becomes flat, we don't get the same rhythm' (Jussawala and Dasenbrock 1992: 85, 86). Yet she writes in English, because, in addition to the difficulties with her native language Igbo, which were mentioned in Chapter 4, most of her readers do not know Igbo. Another female author from Nigeria, Zaynab Alkali, finds writing in English 'agonizing', as her characters in the fictional world do not actually 'speak in English, and in the act of translation, the native idiom is completely lost, as are the meanings of certain expressions' (James 1990: 31). Even Raja Rao, who in spite of finding his own native language Kannada 'never adequate' for writing fiction, wants to write his last novel in the language, as 'there are certain shades and delicacies of expression that aren't available in English' (Jussawala and Dasenbrock 1992: 145).

A similar difficulty in converting lexical items in another language into English is faced by the Singaporean author Catherine Lim. English curse words, for example, are inadequate or inappropriate for Lim's purpose. For her, 'English words like "bloody" or "damn" or the four-letter words just don't capture the spirit of a mother-in-law cursing her daughter's husband, for example' (in Mangan 1998: 7). She also finds English kinship terms inadequate for her purpose. Similarly, Salman Rushdie finds the Urdu word 'sharam' untranslatable, even though it can be translated as 'shame' and appears as the title of one of his novels. Rushdie, however, felt that the Urdu word 'sharam' should also appear on the cover of the book, as it denotes not only shame but also 'embarrassment, discomfiture, decency, modesty, shyness, the sense of having an ordained place in the world, and other dialects of emotion for which English has no counterparts' (1983: 35). More broadly, Achebe has claimed that 'it'd be easier to translate Igbo into music or into the sound of Chinese, than into English.' (Hopkinson 1998: 11). Achebe, however, like his Igbo compatriot Emecheta, writes his creative works in English, not Igbo, and, in spite of the difficulties, there are various occasions when he has to represent in English what was supposed to be originally in Igbo.

Apart from the direct representation in or 'translation' into English, with limited linguistic or cultural appeals to the original language, there are more self-conscious ways by which other languages are represented in English. For example, when conversational Igbo is supposed to be used in Achebe's novels, it is represented in 'a cadenced, proverb-laden style' (Riddy 1970: 39). In Indian writing in English, the writer may at times 'deliberately mangle the English in an attempt at capturing the original ...' (Wood 1997: 33). Likewise, the South African novelist Alan Paton uses certain features of the Zulu language in order to indicate to readers that the dialogue should be in Zulu. In relation to the New Zealand author Patricia Grace, it has been observed that 'Among the stories in *Waiariki* (1975) are some imitations of traditional folktales, and these are told in a quaint style which is meant to look like a literal translation of Maori' (Corballis 1984: 39). This is clear in her story 'And So I Go' (Grace 1975: 47):

Now I stand on a tide-wet rock to farewell the sea. I listen and hear your great heart thud. I hear you cry. Do you too weep for me? Do you reach out with mottled hands to touch *my brow* and anoint my tear-wet face with tears of salt?

The personification of the sea and the character's address to it do seem unusual in English, and are clearly borrowed, almost directly, from Maori. However, the text is enriched by the infusion of Maori elements into English, and the entire story, in fact, could not have been written without these features.

Okara and the (im)possibility of literal translation

One of the most sustained attempts to use English as if it is another language has been made by Gabriel Okara in his novel *The Voice* ([1964] 1970). Okara's work has been described as an attempt 'to handle English not just as a new language, but almost as an extension of his own vernacular' (Izevbaye 1974: 140). He does this through the process of what is called *transliteration*, which has a specific meaning in the Nigerian context: one not only translates, but tries to render the language as literally as possible (see Onwuemene 1999). In this light, Okara (1963: 15) attempts to 'keep as close as possible to the vernacular expressions', by translating almost literally from his native language Ijo. According to Okara (1963: 15), 'In order to capture the vivid images of African speech, I had to eschew the habit of expressing my thoughts first in English'.

The use of Ijo expressions can be seen in the following lines from the beginning of *The Voice* ([1964] 1970: 23): 'Okolo had no chest, they said. His chest was not strong and he had no shadow'. Okara (1963: 15–16) gives a further impression of the flavour of the Ijo language and its underlying logic in the two sentences:

> Some words and espressions ... are rooted in the legends and tales of a far-gone day. Take the expression 'he is timid' for example. The equivalent in Ijaw is 'he has no chest' or 'he has no shadow', Now a person without a chest in the physical sense can only mean a human that does not exist. The idea becomes clearer in the second translation. A person who does not cast a shadow of course does not exist. All this means is that a timid person is not fit to live.

However, Okara's *The Voice* is a unique work. Many other authors have found it difficult to 'translate' from another language into English, even when they attempt to do it to a less holistic extent than in Okara's novel (for a survey of other works in African literature which attempt this technique, see Adejare 1998).

Okara recognises the untranslatability of many Ịjọ expressions iton English very well, as evident in what is said by the character of Chief Izongo in *The Voice* (1970: 45), which can also be seen as a reflection of the limitation of his native audience when English is used:

> You have first heard the spoken words of Abadi and they have entered your ears. He spoke in English and many words missed our ears while many entered our ears. We will not blame him for that for, who among us will not speak thus with such big book learning.

Perhaps the character of Abadi, who is a village elder and adviser to Izongo, is an ironic reflection of Okara's own predicament. However, Abadi has the sympathy of the Chief, who minimises the inappropriateness of his use of English by saying that many of his tribesmen will also 'speak thus with such big book learning', even if 'many words missed our ears'. Abadi's problem can also be related to the more severe problem faced by the main character, Okolo, whose 'head was not correct' because of 'knowing too much book' (Okara 1970: 23).

Going beyond Okara, it must be mentioned that translation is also an important concern in Chinese–American literature, where one of the major themes is the portrayal of 'the difficulties of translation, the impossibility of reaching across borders that appear to be impenetrable by language, by cadences, by culture' (Cutter 1997: 582). So important is this concern in their works that 'translation is not just a specific theme, but is in fact the plot of the works as a whole' (Cutter 1997: 582). Citing the studies of Karlgren (1962) and Aaronson and Ferres (1986), Cutter (1997) explains that as there is an average of ten different meanings corresponding to each Chinese syllable in a small dictionary, Chinese words can have between three to sixteen times as many meanings as English words. Thus 'word meanings in Chinese are radically polysemous; homographs for a word such as "wen," for example, can mean such diverse things as "hear," "smell," or "news" ' (Cutter 1997: 584). The Zimbabwean author Zimunya, in spite of his defence of the use of English against the criticisms of Ngũgĩ (see p. 93), is of the view that 'there are some areas where the English language is too stifling, too inflexible, rigid, and cannot quickly translate the feelings, moods, experiences that we have'. In translating from his mother tongue Shona to English, Zimunya exclaims that 'We only render the meaning, but not the feeling. The feeling is lost. The feeling!' (Williams 1998).

Discourse conventions and styles

Moving beyond the more micro-linguistic features associated with certain languages and how they intermingle, exist side by side or are transposed into English, there are discourse conventions and styles. Some of these conventions or styles are associated with myths, legends, folktales, aphorisms, incantations, tongue twisters and riddles found in the source language. For example, some writers of Yorùbá and Igbo descent have used the styles and conventions associated with their respective native languages in works written in English, which have resulted in the production of 'two distinctive tribal prose styles' in Nigerian literature (Lindfors 1971: 59). Another example from a different part of the world is the Samoan writer Albert Wendt, who has been described as 'the true heir of the Samoan storyteller, the tusitala, in that he can reproduce in dialogue many characteristic modes of speech ...' (Bardolph 1984: 51).

Some of the styles and conventions are closely associated with the source language, and they may be difficult to convey in English as they depend on the phonological resources, sound patterns or the distinctive idiomatic or metaphorical expressions found in the language. Among them are conventions found in some aphorisms, incantations, tongue twisters and riddles. A work in Maori, for example, will have a lot of genealogical references, but this convention does not work well in English. Novels that attempt a virtually word-for-word rendering of the distinctive idiomatic or metaphorical expressions of another language into English, such as Okara's *The Voice*, are rare. Okara's attempt is successful, but one cannot help concluding that, as far as the novel as a genre is concerned, it is a one-off accomplishment that he was not able to repeat in subsequent works, as he produced only one novel.

Conventions that do not intimately depend on the sounds of the language are usually more easily carried over, even if they are closely associated with the non-English language. Sometimes, these conventions are introduced virtually undetected into the work written in English. The persistence of these conventions has been stressed by Gumperz and Cook-Gumperz (1982: 6):

> ... even where the original native language is lost the old discourse conventions tend to persist and to be taken over into the group's use of the majority language. In fact, these conventions come to reflect the identity of the group itself ...

What may be encountered in a work written in English is the clash of discourse conventions, although some readers may not be able to recognise this. For example, a novel may adopt the discourse conventions of the novel as it is written in the West, but it may also assimilate the discourse conventions associated with the author's native culture. The latter, however, may be less obvious, when compared with the conventions of the novel, to readers who do not belong to the same native culture.

Non-linguistic barriers

Language or dialectal variance may not be the only barrier to understanding literatures in English. Although language is an important consideration, especially when there are significant dialectal differences with British English or other Englishes that the reader is familiar with, there are other barriers that may also create difficulties.

Among the most important barriers to understanding are cultural barriers, and these should not be easily discounted or underestimated. A work of literature may be written pretty much in what is regarded as standard British English, but may still defy understanding. For example, William Walsh (1973: 20) has noted that:

> As readers of the Indian novel, non-Indians have their deficiencies. It is hard for a British reader, for instance, to take up the references – to the Indian scene, the agricultural tradition, the vast distances, the terrible poverty, the profoundly significant religion.

The same observation can undoubtedly be made in relation to other literatures in English.

Concluding summary

The English language has come a long way. From a language introduced by invading forces into England after the Roman occupation, it has grown into a world language. It is not only used as a global lingua franca, but internationally works of literature are also written in it. However, its initial spread far beyond England also had to do with invasion, and, in a way, literatures in English cannot sever themselves from their connection with British imperialism. As a residue of colonialism, the standard of what English should be is quite often determined by the mother country, and this is also the case with regard to literature. However, prevailing attitudes to both language and literature are changing.

Language, as argued in the book, plays an important part in the aesthetic realisation of postcolonial literatures. Although language use in postcolonial literatures may be romanticised in the metropolitan centres of learning in the West, it is clear that it often serves a political purpose. This is also seen in contemporary Anglo-Scottish and Anglo-Welsh literatures, which share many of the concerns of postcolonial literatures. The question here is not only what kind of English to use – as in Kelman and Welsh's use of Scots in their works – but also whether English should be used at all, which is R.S. Thomas's dilemma.

Language also plays an important part in the attempt to realise a national identity, and it is a central issue in the literatures of postcolonial America in the nineteenth century and of the other white settler colonies. The literary importance of Mark Twain in the realisation of a distinct national identity, which is primarily realised through language that is significantly different from that used by the English, should be highlighted. However, considering the perception of America as a cultural imperialist force today, the analysis of American postcoloniality may be problematic in other directions. The division between the white settlers and the natives or other minorities in the population is another problem, in relation   not only to America but also to the other white settler colonies. Quite often, this division is manifested in a linguistic divide, or a series of linguistic divides, between English and the other languages.

The question of language continues to be central when one moves beyond the white settler colonies. Quite often, the oral and literate cultures of the colonised communities are negatively affected by the introduction of English. Oral and written literatures in non-English languages are sidelined, and whole languages have disappeared because of the dominance of English and other factors associated with British colonialism. Naturally, the question of whether or why literatures in English should continue to be written is of paramount importance. Ngũgĩ is the major figure who answers this question in the negative, and the significance of his position can be seen in his prominence throughout this book.

However, other writers and scholars disagree with Ngũgĩ and have stressed the view that English can indeed be used. It may in fact be the only or the main language of some authors. Achebe finds it difficult to write in Igbo, because of some problems with the written version of the language, and feels that English is in some ways more of a national language than the other languages spoken in Nigeria. There are writers who propose that a localised variety of the language should be used. Achebe, among many other writers, uses pidgin English in some parts of his work; Brathwaite proposes that Caribbean poetry should resort to *nation language* if the poet wants to represent the language actually spoken in the Caribbean; and Okara boldly experiments with the writing of English as if it were Ịjọ.

Postcolonial literatures in English will continue to grow, perhaps with greater flourish than in England itself. In many ways, the English language and the literatures written in it have long ceased to be the exclusive preserve of the English. The growth of the language and of art works using it, including literature, is undoubtedly aided by the practical value of the language.

Given the dominance of English, one cannot end without sounding a note of caution again. While some people with a vested interest in the English language and its literatures may be happy with their present status, there is serious concern that the world will become more sterile if their growth is at the expense of other languages and literatures. Indeed, the vibrancy of postcolonial literatures in English is heavily dependent on the healthy existence of other languages and cultures. Ngũgĩ's salutary warning about the imperialism of English should therefore be heard and respected, even if we do not entirely agree with him.

Bibliography

Aaronson, D. and Ferres, S (1986) 'Sentence Processing in Chinese-American Bilinguals', *Journal of Memory and Language* 25: 136–62.

Achebe, C. (1960) *No Longer at Ease*, London: Heinemann.

—— (1965) 'English and the African Writer', *Transition* 18: 27–30.

—— (1966) *A Man of the People*, London: Heinemann.

—— (1975) *Morning Yet on Creation Day*, New York: Doubleday.

Adejare, O. (1998) 'Translation: A Distinctive Feature of African Literature in English', in E.L. Epstein and R. Kole (eds) *The Language of African Literature*, Trenton, NJ: Africa World Press.

Aegerter, L.P. (1997) 'Michelle Cliff and the Paradox of Privilege', *College English* 59: 898–915.

Afzal-Khan, F. (1998) 'Interrogating Post-Colonialism: Theory, Text and Context', *World Literature Today* 72: 221–2.

Ahmad, A. (1987) 'Jameson's Rhetoric of Otherness and the "National Allegory" ', *Social Text* 17: 3–25.

—— (1992) *In Theory: Classes, Nations, Literatures*, London: Verso.

Alberto, P.L. (1997) 'Emperor's English: Language as a Technology of Rule in British West Africa', *Penn History Review* 5 (Spring). Online. Available HTTP: http://clio.history.upenn.edu/phr/spring97/ess2.html (May 2000).

Amadi, E.(1965) *The Concubine*, London: Heinemann.

Anand, M.R. (1940) *Untouchable*, London: Penguin Books.

Anderson, B. (1991) *Imagined Communities*, Revised edition, New York: Verso.

Anggraeni, D. (1998) *Journeys through Shadows*, Briar Hill, Victoria: Indra Publishing.

Armitage, D. (1998) 'Literature and Empire', in N. Canny (ed.) *The Oxford History of the British Empire*, vol. 1, Oxford: Oxford University Press.

'Are We Serious About Culture?' *Ghanaian Independent*, *Africa News Service* 16 October 1997.

Ashcroft, B, Griffiths, G. and Tiffin, H. (1989) *The Empire Writes Back*, London: Routledge.

—— (eds) (1995) *The Post-Colonial Studies Reader*, London: Routledge.

Bailey, R.W. (1991) *Images of English: A Cultural History of the Language*, Ann Arbor: University of Michigan Press.

Baker, C. (2000) ' "It's the Same Me, Isn't It?": The Language Question and Brian Fîlel's *Translations', The Midwest Quarterly* 41(3): 264–75.

Barber, K.(1999) 'African-Language Literature and Post-Colonial Criticism', in T.J. Cribb (ed.) *Imagined Commonwealths: Cambridge Essays on Commonwealth and International Literature in English*, Houndsmill: Macmillan Press.

—— and Moraes Farias, P. F. de (1989) 'Introduction', in K. Barber and P. F. de Moraes Farias (eds) *Discourse and its Disguises: The Interpretation of African Oral Texts*, Birmingham: University of Birmingham Centre for West African Studies.

Bandele-Thomas, B. (1991) *The Man Who Came In From the Back of Beyond*, London: Bellew.

Bardolph, J. (1984) 'Albert Wendt: A New Writer from Samoa', in B. Olinder (ed.) *A Sense of Place: Essays in Post-Colonial Literatures*, Gothenburg: Gothenburg University, Commonwealth Studies.

Barnes, J. *et al.* (1998) 'The Man in the Back Row Has a Question V', *Paris Review* 146: 156–79.

Barrett, C. (1947) 'Rolf Boldrewood and His Books', in R. Boldrewood, *Robbery Under Arms*, London: Cassell and Company.

Battersby, E. (1996) 'Saturday Profile – David Malouf; Writer of Mixed Heritage Who Is Quintessentially Australian', *The Irish Times* 25 May: 2.

Bauer, L. (1994) *Watching English Change: An Introduction to the Study of Linguistic Change in Standard Englishes in the Twentieth Century*, London: Longman.

Beckman, S (1981) 'Language as Cultural Identity in Achebe, Ihimaera, Lawrence and Atwood', *World Literature Written in English* 20: 117–38.

Bell, I. (1994) 'Four Letter Truths', *The Observer* (Features: Review) 27 March: 16.

Benjamin, M. (1995) 'The Commonwealth: Pedestal or Pyre? (Interview with Poet and Playwright Derek Walcott)', *New Statesman & Society* 21 July: 30–2.

Benson, P. (1986) *Black Orpheus, Transition, and Modern Cultural Awakening in Africa*, Berkeley: University of California Press.

Bernal, M. (1987) *Black Athena: The Afroasiatic Roots of Classical Civilization*, New Brunswick, NJ: Rutgers University Press.

Bex, T. and Watts, R.J. (eds) (1999) *Standard English: The Widening Debate*, London: Routledge.

Blake, N.F. (1981) *Non-Standard Language in English Literature*, London: André Deutsch.

Boehmer, E. (1995) *Colonial and Postcolonial Literature*, Oxford: Oxford University Press.

Boldrewood, R. [1888] (1947) *Robbery Under Arms*, London: Cassell and Company.

Brathwaite, E.K. (1984). *History of the Voice*. London: New Beacon Books.

—— (1993) *Roots*, Ann Arbor: University of Michigan Press.

Breitinger, E. (ed.) (1996) *Defining New Idioms and Alternative Forms of Expression*, Amsterdam: Rodopi.

Bridgman, Richard (1966) *The Colloquial Style in America*, New York: Oxford University Press.

Brissenden, A. (1972) *Rolf Boldrewood*, Melbourne: Oxford University Press.

Brückner, T. (1996) 'When Europe Came to Africa: The Languages of African Literatures', in Breitinger (ed.) (1996).

Buell, L.E. (1992) 'American Literary Emergence as a Postcolonial Phenomenon', *American Literary History* 4: 411–42.

Bynack, V.P. (1984) 'Noah Webster's Linguistic Thought and the Idea of an American National Culture', *Journal of the History of Ideas* 45: 99–114.

Calder, A. and Wilson, B. (1996) 'Obituary: Sorley Maclean: Poet of the Gaelic World', *The Guardian* 25 November: 11.

'Capturing Working Scots' Idiom' (1997) *Canberra Times* 26 January.

Carey, J. (1996) 'A Turbulent Priest' *Sunday Times* 10 November: 8. Online. Available HTTP: http://www.sunday-times.co.uk/news/pages/sti/1996/11/10/stibooboo01012.html May 2000.

Cartelli, T. (1999) *Repositioning Shakespeare: National Formations, Postcolonial Appropriations*, London: Routledge.

Carter, R. and McRae, J. (1997) *The Routledge History of Literature in English: Britain and Ireland*, London: Routledge.

Chamberlin, J.E. (1993) *Come Back to Me My Language: Poetry and the West Indies*, Urbana and Chicago: University of Illinois Press.

Chinweizu, O.J., and Madubuike, I. (1975) 'Towards the Decolonization of African Literature', *Transition* 48: 29–7, 54, 56–7.

—— (1983). *The Decolonization of African Literature*, vol. 1, Washington: Howard University Press.

Chuah, G.E. (1994) *Echoes of Silence*, Kuala Lumpur: Holograms.

Chukwukere, B.I. (1969) 'The Problem of Language in African Creative Writing', *African Literature Today* 3: 15–26.

Cisneros, S. (1989) *The House on Mango Street*, New York: Vintage Contemporaries.

Clarke, J. (2000) 'Voicing Difference in Language', *Essays on Canadian Writing* Spring: 127–134.

Cliff, M. (1985) *The Land of Look-Behind*, Ithaca: Firebrand Books.

—— (1987) *No Telephone to Heaven*, New York: E.P. Dutton.

Coetzee, J.M. (1988) *White Writing: On the Culture of Letters in South Africa*, New Haven: Yale University Press.

—— (1999) *Disgrace*, London: Secker & Warburg.

Corballis, R. (1984) 'Contemporary Maori Writing in English', in Olinder (ed.) (1984).

Cosgrove, S. (1997) 'Falling foul of the F-word', *The Guardian* 4 August: 22.

Coy, R. (1936) 'A Study of Whitman's Diction', *University of Texas Studies in English* 16: 115–24.

Crawford, R. (1992) *Devolving English Literature*, Oxford: Clarendon Press.

Cribb, T.J. (1999) 'In the Shadow of Language: From Joyce to Okri', in T.J. Cribb (ed.) *Imagined Commonwealths: Cambridge Essays on Commonwealth and International Literature in English*, Houndsmill: Macmillan Press.

Crystal, D. (1997) *English as a Global Language*, Cambridge: Cambridge University Press.

Cutter, M.J. (1997) 'An Impossible Necessity: Translation and the Recreation of Linguistic and Cultural Identities in Contemporary Chinese American Literature', *Criticism* 39: 581–612.

Dabydeen, D. (1984) *Slave Song*, Mundelstrup: Dangaroo Press.

—— (1990) 'On Not Being Milton: Nigger Talk in England Today', in C. Ricks, and L. Michaels (eds) *State of the Language*, London: Faber & Faber.

Daruwalla, K.N. (1980) *Two Decades of Indian Poetry in English 1960–1980*, New Delhi: Vikas Publishing House.

Dathorne, O.R. (1971) 'Amos Tutuola: The Nightmare of the Tribe', in B. King (ed.) *Introduction to Nigerian Literature* Lagos: Evans Brothers.

Dawson, C. and Pfordresher, J. (eds) (1979) *Matthew Arnold, Prose Writings: The Critical Heritage*, London: Routledge and Kegan Paul.

Desai, G. (1993) 'English as an African Language', *English Today* 9 (34): 4–11.

—— (2000) 'Rethinking English: Postcolonial English Studies', in H. Schwartz and S. Ray (eds), *A Companion to Postcolonial Studies*, Malden, MA: Basil Blackwell.

Deshpande, G. (n.d.) *An Anthology of Indian Poetry in English*, Delhi: Hind.

Dharwadker, A. and Dharwadker, V. (1996) 'Language, Identity, and Nation in Postcolonial Indian English Literature', in R. Mohanram and G. Rajan (eds) *English Postcoloniality: Literature from Around the World*, Westport, CT: Greenwood Press.

Dickman, S. (1998) 'An Interview with Shashi Deshpande', *ARIEL* 29(1): 129–35.

Donnell, A. and Welsh, S.L. (eds) (1996) *The Routledge Reader in Caribbean Literature*, London: Routledge.

Donoghue, D. (1997) 'Fears for Irish Studies in an Age of Identity Politics', *Chronicle of Higher Education* 12 November: B4.

Dorian, N.C. (1981) Language Death: *The Life Cycle of a Scottish Gaelic Dialect*, Philadelphia: University of Pennsylvania Press.

Downer, L. (1996) 'The Beats of Edinburgh', *The New York Times* 31 March: 42.

Driver, D. (1996) 'Modern South African Literature in English: A Reader's Guide to Some Recent Critical and Bibliographic Resources', *World Literature Today* 70: 99–106.

Eagleton, T. (1995) *Heathcliff and The Great Hunger: Studies in Irish Culture*, London: Verso.

Edgell, Z. (1982) *Beka Lamb*, London: Heinemann.

Egejuru, P.A. (1978) *Black Writers, White Audience: A Critical Approach to African Literature*, Hicksville, NY: Exposition Press.

Elliott, B. (1974) 'Australia', in B. King (ed.) *Literatures of the World in English*, London: Routledge & Kegan Paul.

Ellison, M. (1994) 'Booker Verdict Upsets Judge', *The Guardian* 12 October: 1.

Ellmann, R. (1982) *James Joyce*, New York: Oxford University Press.

Emecheta, B. (1979) *The Joys of Motherhood*, London: Allison and Busby.

Emenyonu, E. (1978) *The Rise of the Igbo Novel*, Ibadan: Oxford University Press.

Ezekiel, N. (1969) 'Some Additional Comments' in P. Lal, (ed.) *Modern Indian Poetry in English: An Anthology and a Credo*, Calcutta: Writer's Workshop.

Fernando, L. (1997) 'Take On a World with Language', *New Straits Times* (Life and Times Section) 10 December: 8.

Firchow, P. (1995)'The Urgency of Identity: Contemporary English-Language Poetry from Wales' (Book review), *World Literature Today* 69: 591.

Fitzmaurice, S. (1999) 'Aspects of Afrikaans in South African Literature in English', in Cribb (1999a): 166–89.

Fox, R.E. (1998) 'Tribute: Tutuola and the Commitment to Tradition', *Research in African Literatures* 29(3): 203–8.

Fraser, S. (1999) 'Teaching Scots Words When Wlat Disnae', *Scotland on Sunday* 4 July: 6.

Gadd, B. (1999) Review of *The Oxford Book of Modern Australian Verse* (P. Porter) and *Australian Verse: An Oxford Anthology* (J. Leonard), *World Literature Today* 73: 813.

Gallagher, S.M. (1998) 'Letters to the Editor: Irish in Schools', *The Irish Times* 24 September: 15.

Gallagher, S.V. (1997a) 'The Backward Glance: History and the Novel in Post-Apartheid South Africa', *Studies in the Novel* 29: 376–95.

—— (1997b)'Linguistic Power: Encounter with Chinua Achebe', *The Christian Century* 12 March: 260ff.

Gardiner, A. (1987) 'J.M. Coetzee's *Dusklands*: Colonial Encounters of the Robisonian Kind', *World Literature Written in English* 27:174–84.

Gilbert, H. and Tompkins. J. (1996) *Post-Colonial Drama: Theory, Practice, Politics*, London: Routledge.

Gohrbandt, D. (1996) 'The Principle of Inclusiveness: Reflections on Writing and Speaking in Contemporary Nigerian Fiction', in Breitinger (ed.) (1996).

Gordimer, N. and Clingman, S. (1992) 'The Future is Another Country', *Transition* 56: 132–50.

Gordon, E. and Williams, M. (1998) 'Raids on the Articulate: Code-Switching, Style-Shifting and Post-Colonial Writing', *Journal of Commonwealth Literature* 33(2): 75–96.

Granqvist, R. (1984) 'Chinua Achebe's Language: An Examination of Views', in Olinder (ed.) (1984).

Gray, A. (1990). *Something Leather*, London: Jonathan Cape.

Grace, P. (1975) *Waiariki*, Auckland: Longman Paul.

Graddol, D. (1996) 'Global English, Global Culture?' in S. Goodman and D. Graddol (eds) *Redesigning English*, London: Routledge.

Griffiths, G. (1997) 'Writing, Literacy and History in Africa', in M-H. Msiska and P. Hyland (eds) *Writing and Africa*, London: Longman.

Gumperz, J.J. and Cook-Gumperz, J. (1982) *Language and Social Identity*, Cambridge: Cambridge University Press.

Hall, S. (1991a) 'The Local and the Global: Globalization and Ethnicity', in A.D. King (ed.) *Culture, Globalization and the World-System Contemporary Conditions for the Representation of Identity*, Houndmills: Macmillan.

—— (1991b) 'Old and New Identities, Old and New Ethnicities', in A.D. King (ed.) *Culture, Globalization and the World-System Contemporary Conditions for the Representation of Identity*, Houndmills: Macmillan.

Hanks, R. (1997) 'The World's Favourite Language', *The Independent* 16 August: 25.

Harrison, D. (1994) 'Curses! What the ****'s Going On?', *The Observer* 16 October: 9.

Hashmi, A. and Lal, M. (1998) 'Editorial', *ARIEL* 29(1): 7–9.

Helgerson, R. (1998) 'Language Lessons: Linguistic Colonialism, Linguistic Postcolonialism, and the Early Modern English Nation', *Yale Journal of Criticism* 11 (1): 289–99.

Helmi, Y. (1999) 'He's All for Subverting English', *The Straits Times* (Life Section) 8 September: 11.

Hemingway, E. (1954) *Green Hills of Africa*, London: Jonathan Cape.

Heptonstall, G. (1997) 'Furious Interiors of R.S. Thomas', *Contemporary Review* 271, 1581 (October): 215–6. Online. Available HTTP: http://www.britannica.com/bcom/magazine/article/0,5744,224761,00.html (May 2000).

Holmes, J. (1996) 'The Voice Interview: "Just" an Igbo Woman', *The Voice* 9 July. Online. Available HTTP: http://emeagwali.com/nigeria/biography/buchi-emecheta-voice-09jul96.html (May 2000).

Hope, A.D. (1989) 'Standard English: Whose Standard?', in R. K. Dhawan, P. V. Dhamija and A. K. Shrivastava (eds) *Recent Commonwealth Literature*, vol. 1, New Delhi: Prestige Books.

Hopkinson, A. (1998) 'Book Review: "If Something Needs to be Said Right Away, You Don't Put It in a Novel, You Write an Essay" ', *Independent* 20 December: 11.

Huggan, G. (1997) 'Prizing "Otherness": A Short History of the Booker', *Studies in the Novel* 29: 412–33.

Hunter, J. (1997) 'Timelines', in R. Carter and J. McRae (eds) *The Routledge History of Literature in English: Britain and Ireland*, London: Routledge.

Ibrahim, H. (1998) 'Transnational Migrations and the Debate of English Writing in/of Pakistan', *ARIEL* 29(1): 33–48.

Izevbaye, D.S. (1974) 'Nigeria', in B. King (ed.) *Literatures of the World in English*, London: Routledge & Kegan Paul.

Jack, I. (1997) 'Nation Shall Speak unto Nation', *The Guardian* (Feature) 27 November: 1.

Jaggi, M. (1998) 'Speaking in Tongues', *The Guardian* 18 July: T026.

James, A. (1990) 'Interview with Zaynab Alkali', in *In Their Own Voices: African Women Writers Talk*, London: Heinemann.

James, L. (2000) *Caribbean Literature in English*, London: Longman.

Jeffares, A.N. (1974) 'Ireland', in in B. King (ed.) *Literatures of the World in English*, London: Routledge & Kegan Paul.

Jefiyo, B. (1989) 'On Eurocentric Critical Theory: Some Paradigms from the Texts and Sub-Texts of Post-Colonial Writing', *Kunapipi* 11(1): 107–18.

—— (1990) 'The Nature of Things: Arrested Decolonization and Critical Theory', *Research in African Literature* 21: 33–48.

Jenkins, E. (1997) 'To Be Welsh or Not To Be' [Review of *D. Abse* (ed.) Twentieth-Century Anglo-Welsh Poetry], *Times* 11 September: 30. Online. Available HTTP: http://www.the-times.co.uk/news/pages/tim/1997/09/11/timfeabks01002.html (May 2000).

Jenkins, S. (1997) 'The Bards of the Byrger', *Times* 6 August: 16.

Johnstone, G. (1967) 'The Language of Australian Literature', *Australian Literary Studies* 3: 18–27.

Jolly, R. (1995) 'Rehearsal of Liberation: Contemporary Post-colonial Discourse and the New South Africa', *PMLA* 110: 17–29.

Jones, R.F. (1953) *The Triumph of the English Language*, Stanford: Stanford University Press.

Joyce, J. [1916] (1960) *Portrait of the Artist as a Young Man*, Harmondsworth: Penguin Books.

Jury, L. (1997) 'It's Too Late for My Beloved Wales', *The Independent* 14 September: 3.

Jussawala, F. and Dasenbrock, R.W. (1992) *Interviews with Writers of the Postcolonial World*, Jackson: University Press of Mississippi.

Kachru, B.B. (1986) *The Alchemy of English*, Oxford: Pergamon.

—— (1995) 'The Speaking Tree: A Medium of Plural Canons', in M. L. Tickoo (ed.) *Language and Culture in Multilingual Societies*, Singapore: SEAMEO Regional Language Centre.

Karlgren, B. (1962) *Sound and Symbol in Chinese*, Hong Kong: Hong Kong University Press.

Karim, N. A. (1998) 'The Changing Face of Indo-Anglian Literature', *The Hindu* 1 February.

Karrer, W. and Lutz, H. (1990) 'Minority Literatures in North America: From Cultural Nationalism to Liminality', in W. Karrer and H. Lutz (eds) *Minority Literatures in North America: Contemporary Perspectives*, Frankfurt: Peter Lang.

Kavoori A.P. (1998) 'Getting Past the Latest "Post": Assessing the Term "Post-Colonial" ', *Critical Studies in Mass Communication* 15: 195–203.

Kelman, J. (1997) 'Obituary: Amos Tutuola: Weaver of Fantasy', *The Guardian* 16 June: 13.

—— [1994] (1998) *How Late It Was, How Late*, London: Vintage.

Keneally, T. (1972) *The Chant of Jimmie Blacksmith*, Sydney: Angus & Robertson.

Kennedy, A.L. (1996) 'Scots to the Death', *The New York Times* 20 July: 19.

Kennedy, A.L. and Taylor, D.J. (1996) 'Head to Head: Written Out of the Plot', *The Guardian* 28 September: 4.

Kiberd, D. (1999) 'The Empire Writes Back – Once the British and French sent Novels as Well as Governors to the Four Corners of the Globe...', *Irish Times* 10 August: 10.

King, A.D. (ed.) (1991) *Culture, Globalization and the World-System Contemporary Conditions for the Representation of Identity*, Houndmills: Macmillan.

King, B. (1974) 'Introduction', in B. King (ed.) *Literatures of the World in English*, London: Routledge & Kegan Paul.

—— (1992) 'Introduction', in B. King (ed.) *Post-Colonial English Drama: Commonwealth Drama since 1960*, New York: St Martin's Press.

Krebs, P.M. (1997) 'Olive Schreiner's Racialization of South Africa', *Victorian Studies* 40: 427–44.

Kunene, M. (1968) 'Deculturation: The African Writer's Response', *Africa Today* 15(4): 19–25.

—— (1996) 'Some Aspects of South African Literature (South African Literature in Transition)', *World Literature Today* 70: 13–16.

Lal, P. and Rao, K.R. (1959) *Modern Indo-Anglian Poetry*. Delhi: Kavita.

Lamming, G. (1992) *The Pleasures of Exile*, Ann Arbor: University of Michigan Press.

Laqueur, W. (1995) 'Once More with Feeling (Postmodernism and Millennialism)', *Society* 33(1): 32–41.

Lawton, D. (1980) 'Language Attitude, Discreteness, and Code-Shifting in Jamaican English', *English World-Wide* 1–2: 211–26.

Lelyveld, D. (1993) 'The Fate of Hindustani: Colonial Knowledge and the Project of a National Language', in C. Breckenbridge and P. van der Veer (eds) *Orientalism and the Postcolonial Predicament: Perspectives on South Asia*, Philadelphia: University of Pennsylvania Press.

Leslie, A. (1998) 'Patriotism without Prejudice', *The Times of London* 30 May: 22. Online. Available HTTP: http://www.the-times.co.uk/news/pages/tim/1998/05/30/timopnope01002.html (May 2000).

Lindfors, B. (1971) 'Characteristic of Yoruba and Igbo Prose Styles in English', in A. Rutherford (ed.) *Common Wealth*, Aarhus: Akademisk Boghandel.

Loomba, A. (1998) *Colonialism/Postcolonialism*, London: Routledge.

Lucas, J. (1990) *England and Englishness: Ideas of Nationhood in English Poetry*, London: Hogarth.

Lutz H. (1997) 'Canadian Native Literature and the Sixties: A Historical And Bibliographical Survey', *Canadian Literature* 152/153: 167–91.

McAlpine, J. (1996) 'Hard Sellers Buy into Soft Scots Accents', *Sunday Times* 9 June.

Macaulay, T.B. (1952) 'Minute on Indian Education (2 February 1835)', in G.M. Young (ed.) *Macaulay: Prose and Poetry*, London: Rupert Hart-Davis.

McCord, A. (1993) 'Black Man's Burden: A Conversation with Mongane Wally Serote', *Transition* 61: 180–87.

McCrum, R., Cran, W. and MacNeil, R. (1986) *The Story of English*, London: Faber & Faber.

MacDiarmid, H. (1978) *Complete Poems 1920–1976*, vol. 1, M. Grieve and W.R. Aitken (eds), London: Matin Brian & O'Keefe.

McGuirk, C. (1985) *Robert Burns and the Sentimental Era*, Athens, Georgia: University of Georgia Press.

McKay, R. (1996) 'Would the Real Irvine Welsh Shoot Up?', *The Observer* (Features) 4 February: 9.

McLellan, J. (1994) 'Word Breaks', *The Guardian* (Letters to the editor) 29 October: 28.

McLuhan, M. (1962) *The Gutenberg Galaxy: The Making of Typographic Man*, London: Routledge and Kegan Paul.

McRae, J. (1991) 'Maori Literature: A Survey', in T. Sturm (ed.) *The Oxford History of New Zealand Literature in English*, Auckland: Oxford University Press.

Maher, J.C. (1998) 'Cultural Insights: In Ireland, A Language Reborn through the Population Change', *The Daily Yomiuri* 16 March: 15.

Mair, C. (1996) 'The Treasures of Whose Tongue? The Language Issue in Caribbean Fiction', E. Breitinger (ed.) *Defining New Idioms and Alternative Forms of Expression*, Amsterdam: Rodopi.

MalmKjær, K. (1999) 'Language and Literature: Englishes and Translation', in T.J. Cribb (ed.) *Imagined Commonwealths: Cambridge Essays on Commonwealth and International Literature in English*, Houndsmill: Macmillan Press.

Malouf, D. (1994) *Remembering Babylon*, London: Vintage.

Mangan, J. (1998) 'Too Sexy for Singapore, It's The Curse of The Romantic', *The Age (News)* 26 August: 7.

Marrin, M. (1998) 'The English Empire Arundhati Roy's Novel is in English Because English is Her Element ...', *The Daily Telegraph* 18 June: 26.

Marchand, P. 'Can Authenticity Flourish Within Boundaries? All My Relations: An Anthology of Contemporary Canadian Native Fiction' *Toronto Star* (Magazine) 25 August: 3.

Martini, J., Rutherford, A., Petersen, K.H., Stenderup, V. and Thomsen, B. (1981) Interview with Ngũgĩ, *Kunapipi* 3(1): 110–6.

Massie, A. (1998) 'Why We Should Get Rid of the Old Emotional Confusion and Live in Harmony Under The Union', *Daily Mail* 14 November: 12.

Mays, M. (1998) '*Finnegans Wake*, Colonial Nonsense, and Postcolonial History' *College Literature* 25(3): 20–34.

Mazrui, A.A. (1966) 'The English Language and Political Consciousness', *Journal of Modern African Studies* 4(3): 295–311.

—— (1975) *The Political Sociology of the English Language*, The Hague: Mouton.

Mazrui, A.A. and Mazrui, A.M. (1998a) *The Power of Babel: Language & Governance in the African Experience*, Oxford: James Currey.

—— (1998b) 'Language in a Multicultural Context: The African Experience', in Mazrui and Mazrui (1998a).

Mazrui, A.M. (1998) 'Linguistic Eurocentricism & African Counter-Penetration: Ali Mazrui & the Global Frontiers of Language, in A.A. Mazrui and A.M. Mazrui *The Power of Babel: Language & Governance in the African Experience*, Oxford: James Currey.

Mencken, H. L. (1974) *The American Language; An Inquiry into the Development of English in the United States* [1919–48], New York: Alfred A. Knopf.

Miller, J. (1998). 'Devolution Revolution; Are Swells of Politics and Pride Breaking Up the United Kingdom?', *The Washington Post* 18 October: C01.

Mo, T. (1983) *Sour Sweet*, London: Abacus.

Mohanty, S. (1997) 'Freedom and the Indian Diaspora', *The Hindu* 21 December.

Moore, C. (2000) 'Choosing Her Words Carefully', *The Press* 24 June: 20.

Moore, G. (1969) *The Chosen Tongue*, London: Longman.

Moss, J. (1996) 'Multiculturalism and Postmodern Theater: Staging Quebec's Otherness', *Mosaic: A Journal for the Interdisciplinary Study of Literature* 29(3): 75–96.

Mufwene, S.S. (2001) *The Ecology of Language Evolution*, Cambridge: Cambridge University Press.

Mukherjee, M. (1996) 'Interrogating Postcolonialism', in H. Trivedi and M. Mukherjee (eds) *Interrogating Postcolonialism: Theory, Text, Context*, Delhi: Indian Institute of Advanced Study.

Murdoch, W. and Mulgan, A. (eds) (1950) *A Book of Australian and New Zealand Verse*, Melbourne: Oxford University Press.

Naipaul, V.S. (1972) *The Overcrowded Barracoon and Other Articles*, London: André Deutsch.

Nandy, P. (1973) *Indian Poetry in English Today*, New Delhi: Sterling.

Narayan, R.K. (1965) 'English in India', in J. Press (ed.) *Commonwealth Literature: Unity and Diversity in a Common Culture*, London: Heinemann.

—— (1978) *The Painter of Signs*, New York: The Viking Press.

—— (1988) *A Writer's Nightmare*, Harmondsworth: Penguin Books.

Neil, A. (1998) 'Scotland the Self-Deluded', *Spectator* 15 August: 11.

Ngũgĩ wa Thiong'o (1986) *Decolonizing the Mind: The Politics of Language in African Literature*, London: Currey.

—— (1998) *Penpoints, Gunpoints and Dreams: Towards a Critical Theory of the Arts and the State in Africa*, Oxford: Clarendon Press.

—— (2000) 'Europhonism, Universities, and the Magic Fountain: The Future of African Literature and Scholarship', *Research in African Literatures* 31(1): 1–11.

Norton, C.E. (1855) Review of *Leaves of Grass*, *Putnam's Monthly* 6 September: 321–23.

Nwoga, D.I. (1990) 'Bilingualism and Literary Creativity', in W. Zach (ed.) *Literature(s) in English: New Perspectives*, Frankfurt: Peter Lang.

O Drisceoil, P. (1997) 'In Pursuit of the Deus Absconditus: Autobiographies by R.S. Thomas', *The Irish Times* (Supplement) 5 July: 9.

Ojo-Ade, F. (1989) *On Black Culture*, Ife-Ife: Obafemi Awolowo University Press.

Okara, G. (1963) 'African Speech, English Words', *Transition* 10: 15–16.

—— [1964] (1970) *The Voice*, London: Heinemann.

Okonkwo, J.I. (1976) 'African Literature and Its Language of Expression', *Africa Quarterly* 15(4): 56–66.

—— (1979) 'The Missing Link in African Literature', *African Literature Today* 10: 86–105.

Olaniyan, T. (2000) 'Africa: Varied Colonial Legacies', in H. Schwartz and S. Ray (eds) *A Companion to Postcolonial Studies*, Malden, MA: Basil Blackwell.

Olinder, B. (ed.) (1984) *A Sense of Place: Essays in Post-Colonial Literatures*, Gothenburg: Gothenburg University, Commonwealth Studies.

Omole, J.O. (1998) Code Switching in Soyinka's *The Interpreters*, in E.L. Epstein and R. Kole (eds) *The Language of African Literature*, Trenton, NJ: Africa World Press.

Onwuemene, M.C. (1999) 'Limits of Transliteration: Nigerian Writers' Endeavors toward a National Literary Language' *PMLA* 114: 1055–66.

'Our Language Destined to be Universal', (1855) *The United States Democratic Review* 35, 4 (April): 306–13. Online. Available HTTP: http://cdl.library.cornell.edu/cgi-bin/moa/sgml/moa-idx?notisid=AGD1642-0035-59 (May 2000).

Parthasarathy, R. (ed.) (1976) *Ten Twentieth-Century Indian Poets*, New Delhi: Oxford University Press.

Parry, T. (1955) *A History of Welsh Literature*, H.I. Bell (trans.). Oxford: Clarendon Press.

Pennycook, A. (1998) *English and the Discourses of Colonialism*. London: Routledge.

Philip, M.N. (1990) 'The Absence of Writing or How I Almost Became a Spy', in C.B. Davies and E.S. Fido (eds), *Out of the Kumbla: Caribbean Women and Literature*. Trenton, NJ: Africa World Press.

Podhoretz, N. (1959) 'The Literary Adventures of Huck Finn', *The New York Times* 6 December: 5.

Preston, Y, (1990) 'Last Chance for Australia's Dying Tongues', *Sydney Morning Herald* 27 October: 21.

Quarcoo, E. (1994) 'The English Language as a Modern Ghanaian Artifact', *Journal of Black Studies* 24: 329–43.

Rahv, P. (1939) 'Paleface and Redskin', *Kenyon Review* 6. 251–56.

Rajan, B. (1974) 'India', in B. King (ed.) *Literatures of the World in English*, London: Routledge & Kegan Paul.

Ramchand, K. (1974) 'The West Indies', in B. King (ed.) *Literatures of the World in English*, London: Routledge & Kegan Paul.

—— (1988) 'West Indian Literary History: Literariness, Orality and Periodization' *Callaloo* 34: 95–110.

Ramnarayan, G. (2000) 'Word for Word' *The Hindu* 7 May.

Rao, R. (1963) 'Author's Foreword', in *Kanthapura*, New York: New Directions.

Reagan, T.G. (1987) 'The Politics of Linguistic Apartheid: Language Policion in South Africa', *Journal of Negro Education* 56: 299–312.

Rhys, J. (1962) 'Let Them Call it Jazz', in *Tigers are Better Looking*, London, André Deutsch.

—— [1966] (1968) *Wide Sargasso Sea*, Harmondsworth: Penguin Books.

Riddy, F (1970) 'Language as a Theme in *No Longer at Ease*', *Journal of Commonwealth Literature* 9: 38–47.

Rodríguez, E.J. (1996) 'Oral Tradition and the New Literary Canon in Recent Caribbean Poetry Anthologies', in Breitinger (ed.) (1996).

Rogers, B. (1997) 'A Bizarre Enterprise', *The Spectator* 279 (8821): 31.

Rushdie, S. (1983) *Shame*, London: Jonathan Cape.

—— (1991) *Imaginary Homelands: Essays And Criticism, 1981–1991*, New York: Viking.

—— (1995) *The Moor's Last Sigh*, London: Vintage.

—— (1997a) 'Introduction', in S. Rushdie and E. West (eds) *The Vintage Book of Indian Writing, 1947–1997*, London: Vintage.

—— (1997b) 'Notes on Writing and the Nation (May 1997 "Index on Censorship" Excerpt)' *Harper's Magazine* 295(1768): 22–4.

Sage, A. (1996) 'Gallic Pop Silences Brits in Funless France', *The Observer* (Overseas news) 18 February: 23.

Saldívar, J.D. (1997) 'Tracking English and American Literary and Cultur', *Daedalus* 126(1): 155–74.

Sanborn, G. (1998) *The Sign of the Cannibal: Melville and the Making of a Postcolonial Reader*, Durham, NC: Duke University Press.

Saro-Wiwa, K. (1985) *Sozaboy: A Novel in Rotten English*, Port Harcourt: Saros International Publishers.

—— (1989) *Four Farcical Plays*, London: Saros International Publishers.

Scammell, W. (1998) 'Books: Needed: Critical Svengalis and Mad Ezras', *The Independent* 18 October: 13.

Selvon, S. [1956] (1972) *The Lonely Londoners*, London: Longman.

—— (1982) 'Sam Selvon Talking – A Conversation with Kenneth Ramchand', *Canadian Literature* 95: 56–64.

—— (1987) 'Finding West Indian Identity in London', *Kunapipi* 9(3): 34–8.

Sherlock, P. (1966) *West Indies*, London: Thames & Hudson.

Shields, T. (1996) 'Whit Ur They Embra Effen Bees Oan Aboot?', *Guardian* 18 May: 27.

S. H. (1853) 'Jacob Grimm on the Genius and Vocation of the English Language' *Notes and Queries* 171 February 5: 125–6.

Shome, R. (1998) 'Caught in The Term "Post-Colonial": Why the "Post-Colonial" Still Matters', *Critical Studies in Mass Communication* 15: 203–12.

Simpson, D. (1986) *The Politics of American English, 1776–1850*, New York: Oxford University Press.

Skinner, J. (1998) *The Stepmother Tongue*, London: Macmillan.

'A Song of Lost Islands (West Indian Writers)' (1994) *The Economist* 10 December: 93.

Soyinka, W. (1975) 'Neo-Tarzanism: The Poetics of Pseudo-Tradition', *Transition* 48: 38–44.

—— (1976) 'We Africans Must Speak with One Tongue', *Afrika* 20: 23.

Taiwo, O. (1976) *Culture And The Nigerian Novel*, New York: St Martin's Press.

Talib, I.S. (1992) 'Why Not Teach Non-Native English Literature?', *The English Language Teaching Journal* 46: 51–5.

—— (1994) 'Responses to the Language of Singaporean Literature in English', in S. Gopinathan, A. Pakir, W.K. Ho and V. Saravanan (eds) *Language, Society and Education in Singapore: Issues and Trends*, Singapore: Times Academic Press.

—— (1996) 'Nonnative English Literature and the World Literature Syllabus', in M. Carroll (ed.) *No Small World: Visions and Revisions of World Literature*, Urbana, Illinois: National Council of Teachers of English.

—— (1998) 'Singaporean Literature in English,' in L. Alsagoff et al (eds) *English in New Cultural Contexts: Reflections from Singapore*, Singapore: Oxford University Press.

—— (1999) 'The Language of Singapore Poetry', in K. Singh (ed.) *Interlogue: Studies in Singapore Literature*, vol. 2: *Poetry*, Singapore: Ethos Books.

Teo, Hsu-Ming (2000) *Love and Vertigo*, St Leonards, NSW: Allen & Unwin.

Thomas, N. (1971) 'An Introduction to Saunders Lewis', in A. Rutherford (ed.) *Common Wealth*, Aarhus: Akademisk Boghandel.

Thomas, R.S. (1993) *Collected Poems 1945–1990*, London: Dent.

Thompson, P. (1998) 'Quest to Find What Lies at the Heart of England', *Waikato Times* 28 April: 6.

Tiffin, H. (1989) 'Post-Colonial Literatures and Counter-Discourse', in D. Riemenschneider (ed.) *Critical Approaches to the New Literatures in English*, Essen. Verlag die Blaue Eule.

Todorov, T [1974] (1987) *The Conquest of America: The Question of the Other*, D. Howard (trans.), New York: Harper Torchbooks.

Tranter, J. (1996) 'Australian Poetry 1940–1980: A Personal View' *Poetry* 169(1): 86–93.

Traugott, E. C. and Pratt, M. L. (1980) *Linguistics for Students of Literature*, New York: Harcourt Brace Jovanovich.

Trilling, L. (1951) *The Liberal Imagination*, London: Secker & Warburg.

Trudgill, P. and Hannah, J. (1994) *International English: A Guide to Varieties of Standard English*, Third edition, London: Arnold.

Tuwhare, H. (1993) *Deep River Talk: Collected Poems*, Auckland: Godwit Press.

Twain, M. [1874] (1943) *The Adventures of Huckleberry Finn*, in *Tom Sawyer and Huckleberry Finn*, London: J.M. Dent.

Viljoen, L. (1996) 'Postcolonialism and Recent Women's Writing in Afrikaans (South African Literature in Transition)', *World Literature Today* 70: 63–72

Viswanathan, G. (1989) *Masks of Conquest: Literary Study and British Rule in India*, New York: Columbia University Press.

Walcott, D. (1965) *The Castaway, And Other Poems*, London: Jonathan Cape.

—— (1980) *Pantomime*, in *Remembrance and Pantomime: Two Plays*, New York: Farrar, Strauss and Giroux.

—— (1986) *Beef, No Chicken*, in *Three Plays*, New York: Farrar, Strauss and Giroux.

Wali, O. (1963) 'The Dead End of African Literature?', *Transition* 10: 13–15.

Walder, D. (1998) *Post-Colonial Literatures in English: History, Language, Theory*, Oxford: Basil Blackwell.

Walsh, W. (1973) *Commonwealth Literature*, Oxford: Oxford University Press.

Ward, G. (1987) *Wandering Girl*, Broome, West Australia: Magabala Press.

Warley, L. (1998) 'Unbecoming a "Dirty Savage": Jane Willis's *Geniesh: An Indian Girlhood*', *Canadian Literature* 156: 83–103.

'The Way We Are' (1993) *The Guardian* (Features) 28 July: 3.

Weisbuch, R. (1986) *Atlantic Double-Cross: American Literature and British Influence in the Age of Emerson*, Chicago. University of Chicago Press.

Welsh, I. [1993] (1996) *Trainspotting*, London: Minerva.

West, A. (1953) 'Shadow and Substance', *The New Yorker* 5 December: 222–3.

Westley, D. (1992) 'Choice of Language and African Literature: A Bibliographic Essay', *Research in African Literatures* 23(1): 159–71.

Whitman, W. [1855] (1982a) *Leaves of Grass*, in *Complete Poetry and Collected Prose*, New York: Viking Press.

—— [1888] (1982b) 'Slang in America', in *Complete Poetry and Collected Prose*, New York: Viking Press.

Widdowson, H.G. (1994) 'The Ownership of English', *TESOL Quarterly* 29: 317–88.

Wilkinson, J. (ed.) (1992) *Talking with African Writers: Interviews by Jane Wilkinson*, London and Portsmouth: James Currey and Heinemann.

Williams, A.A. (1998) 'Mother Tongue: Interviews with Musaemura B. Zimunya and Solomon Mutswairo', *The Journal of African Travel-Writing* 4: 36–44. Online. Available HTTP: http://www.unc.edu/~ottotwo/mothertongue.html (May 2000).

Willis, J. (1973) *Geneish: An Indian Girlhood*, Toronto: New Press.

Wong, N. (1996) 'The English Novel in the Twentieth Century, 4: The Indian Novel in England', *Contemporary Review* 268(1563): 198–201.

Wood, J. (1994) 'In Defence of Kelman', *The Guardian* (Books: Features) 25 October: 9.

—— (1996) 'Letter From Edinburgh', *Newsday* 4 August: 34.

—— (1997) 'An Indelicate Balance: The Noisy Pluralism of Indian Fiction', *The New Republic* 217, 26, 29 December: 32–36.

Wroe, N. (1997) 'King of the Castle', *The Guardian* 25 July: 12.

Yancy, G. (1996) 'U.S. Founders Began Suppression of Our African Speech Patterns', *Philadelphia Tribune* 31 December: 7-A.

Young, P. (1971) 'Mechanism to Medium: The Language of West African Literature in English', in A. Rutherford (ed.) *Common Wealth*, Aarhus: Akademisk Boghandel.

—— (1973) 'Tradition, Language and the Reintegration of Identity in West African Literature in English', in E. Wright (ed.) *The Critical Evaluation of African Literature*, London: Heinemann.

Zapata, J.V. (1996) 'This Is the Voice of Society: The Influence of New Forms of Collective/Mass Communication in the Works of V.S. Naipaul', in Breitinger (1996).

Zinn, C. (2000) 'Obituary: Judith Wright: Australian Poet Who Championed Aboriginal Rights and Environmental Issues' *The Guardian* (29 June). Online. Available HTTP: http://www.guardian.co.uk/Archive/Article/0,4273,4034767,00.html (April 2001).

Zwerdling, A. (1998) *Improvised Europeans: American Literary Expatriates and the Siege of London*, New York: Basic Books.

Index